How to Trade a Range

Trade the Most Interesting Market in the World

Heikin Ashi Trader

DAO PRESS

Imprint

Copyright © 2017 by Heikin Ashi Trader

All rights reserved. No part of this book may be reproduced or utilized in any form or by any means, electronic or mechanical, including photocopying, recording, or by any information storage and retrieval system, without written permission of the publisher.

First edition, October 2017

The information presented herein represents the view of the author as of the date of publication. This book is presented for informational and entertainment purposes only. Due to the rate at which economic and cultural conditions change, the author reserves the right to alter and update his opinions based on new conditions. While every attempt has been made to verify the information in this book, neither the author nor his affiliates/partners assume any responsability for errors, inaccuracies, or omissions. At no time shall the information contained herein be constructed as professional, investment, tax, accounting, legal or medical advice. This book does not constitute a recommendation or a warrant of suitability for any particular business, industry, website, security, portfolio of securities, transaction, or investment strategy.

Published by:

DAO Press, LLC

Plaza de San Cristobal, 14

03002 Alicante

Spain

Table of Contents

1. Introduction to Range Trading............................ 5
2. What Is a Range Market?................................. 13
3. Look to the left! 18
4. How Do I Draw Proper Support and Resistance Lines?.. 23
5. In Which Markets Can You Operate Range Trading?.. 27
   - Currencies... 28
   - *Stocks 28
   - Futures 29
6. How to Trade a Range in Practice 31
7. Where Should I Place the Stop?......................... 45
8. Questions of Trade Management 50
   - A. Should You Close the Trade Before the Weekend? 50
   - B. Should You Use Trailing Stops When Range Trading? 51
   - C. What Should You Do if the Trade Goes "nowhere"?... 52
   - D. Should I Push the Stop Closer to the Market? 52
9. Examples of Range Markets 55

- A. Trading Ranges in the Foreign Exchange Market 55
- B. Deeper Examination of a Sideways Period in the E-Mini 62
- C. Deeper Examination of a Sideways Period in the FDAX 67
- 10. Advanced Strategies 76
  - A. Opportunistic Limits 76
  - B. Fakeouts 84
- 11. Trend Channels (Channel Trading) 87
- 12. What Is Really Important 93
- 13. Range Trading for Day Traders and Scalpers . 96
- Glossary 105
- Other Books by Heikin Ashi Trader 111
- About the Author 115

1. Introduction to Range Trading

Traders usually speak of trend markets and "trendless" markets when characterizing market conditions. It then appears that they earn money when a market is in a trend and should avoid trendless markets, because here there is nothing to write home about.

This view is the logical consequence of a market philosophy, which observes the behavior of financial markets mainly on the appearance of trends. This is, in my opinion, a point of view that traders should question. What traders perceive as "trends" on a chart are often no more than rare anomalies.

The rule is that financial markets are predominantly trading in trendless zones, which are difficult to define. It seems market participants take a wait-and-see attitude at such times. It is true that here, too, contracts change the owners, which can cause some volatility. However, these transactions are not big enough to trigger a significant movement that traders can identify as a "trend."

Traders buy and sell as always, but they do it at prices at which the market players seem to be unanimous. There are also highs and lows, but these are limited even if the trader can identify them on the chart. These extremes then form the lowest or highest prices the market participants are willing to pay. When prices reach these extremes, the trader observes that the market tends to make a 180-degree turn and run toward the other extreme.

In trader language, we speak in this case of a **sideways market** or a **trading range**. Since most traders are trend-oriented, they avoid such market phases or close positions as the market moves into such a phase. Then they wait until the next "signal" comes. These traders hope that the market will move and take up the previous trend again.

I do not want to criticize this way of thinking. It is a legitimate and possibly profitable trading philosophy, which, of course, works particularly well when markets are predominantly in a trend modus. However, if this does not occur, the trend trader has difficulties achieving his goals.

To illustrate the problem more closely, a simple look at the currency pair EUR/USD says enough.

Image 1: EUR/USD, daily chart, May 2015 to October 2016

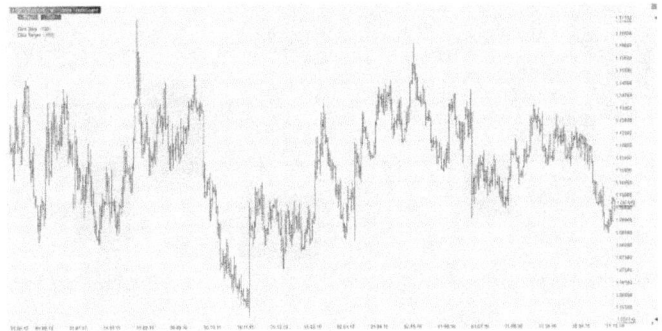

The picture shows the trading of the EUR/USD in a period of about 16 months. Undoubtedly, there were downward or upward trend movements from which a trader could have traded profitably. Looking more closely, however, one quickly realizes that the pair was not in a trend movement for most of the time, but simply traded sideways.

I have marked some of these sideways periods in the chart in yellow. If you counted the number of trading days in which the market was in this "trendless mode," you would quickly find it was the overwhelming majority of the days. In other words, trends are the exceptions, while sideways markets are the rule.

Now some readers could accuse me of deliberately selecting a sideways phase in the EUR/USD.

Image 2: EUR/USD, daily chart, June 2014 to February 2015

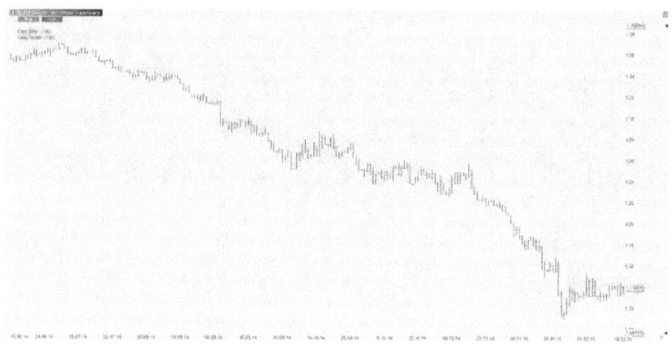

Anyone looking at the period June 2014–February 2015 in the EUR/USD will undoubtedly see a "trend" clearly pointing downward. This is hard to deny. Looking more closely, however, one can see that the EUR/USD also went sideways on most trading days (yellow zones in the chart). The days when the market clearly went in the trend direction form the minority.

Seen from the bird's perspective, the market players seem to drive the pair downward. They sell the euro and buy the dollar. For this orientation to really pay off, however, as a trader you need the proper amount of patience. In some of these sideways periods during this "trend," it took more than a month before the market moved back in the desired direction.

When you are an investor or a trader who acts in the medium or long term, you can rely on this appreciation of the dollar and sit out such a phase confidently. However, the question is: can you do this as a short-term trader who wants to earn money by trading currencies?

Despite this apparent finding, most short-term trading strategies rely on the trend-following model, although it is demonstrably difficult to implement. Most traders I know are more or less looking for a bigger move. Whether they call themselves a day trader, scalper, or whatever.

In the evening (or on the weekend), when everything is said and done on the market, traders are wondering why they have not managed to take this or that move by day, although it appears obvious by looking at the chart.

They do this because they assume they will best meet their financial goals if they could catch one of these larger moves every now and then. Then, they say, "I will be successful as a trader."

At the same time, small, specialized groups of traders exist who do not care about these trends but do exactly the opposite: they trade the trendless phases. It is comprehensible. If you look at a financial chart as a beginner, your eye first falls on the big movements, which are taking place from time to time. In addition, beginners ask themselves:

what do I need to do to benefit from such a movement?

Interestingly, the vast majority of trading literature also deals mainly with the detection of trends. This applies not only to the books that explicitly refer to trend following, but also to most of the books about intraday trading. Although short-term trading is a different game than trend following or investing, it is mostly about how to catch the "big" intraday moves. When you talk with day traders, you realize that most of them are spending their time looking for this kind of market movement.

However, there is an alternative to this type of trend hunting. I call it **range trading**, although it can appear in quite different variants. Before I started writing this book, I consulted trading literature for what other traders had to say about this topic. Interestingly enough, there was almost no book dealing explicitly with this topic, although trading ranges or sideways markets are proven to account for over 70% of the market time!

The only book that refers explicitly to this subject is one by Al Brooks with this somewhat bulky title: *Trading Price Action Trading Ranges: technical Analysis of Price Charts Bar by Bar for the Serious Trader*. It was published in 2012 by Wiley. Brooks describes how to trade pullbacks and breakouts from the range, but how to trade the range itself is quickly checked off in three short chapters.

As you can see, the trend following model has burned so deeply into most traders' brain that they cannot think otherwise.

To remedy this shortcoming, I decided to write this book. It is not about how to identify a range and then trade the breakout from it, but <u>how to trade the range itself.</u>

I would like to point out that this is a very valid and highly interesting trading strategy. I do not intend to treat the topic in an exhaustive way. The idea that sideways markets might even be more interesting than trend markets has only come gradually to my mind. I was fascinated by trends and wanted to profit as much as possible from them. It became clear to me after a while that trend trading is not as easy as it appeared at first glance. However, I did not really have a solution to this problem. I just went looking for other ways or strategies to "trade the trend." And, there are thousands of them.

However, regarding how to trade a range market itself, it is hard to find any literature on this topic (actually none). Every now and then, you can find a page on the Internet that deals with this. Unfortunately, those authors repeat the same slogan: the trader should buy the support and sell the resistance. Well roared, lion!

But how do you identify support and resistance? How do you draw support lines and resistance lines correctly for the range to be identifiable? What signals should the trader take and which ones should he rather avoid? How and where does he get out of the range? And what should he do if the trade does not hit the price target?

These are the real trader questions, and this book deals extensively with them. I wish the reader a good time reading!

2. What Is a Range Market?

Image 3: Range Market

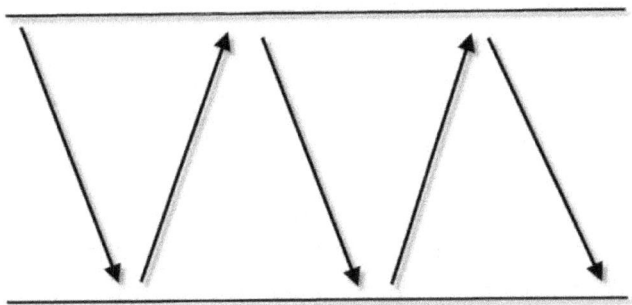

Image 3 shows, simply sketched, what a range market is all about. The price moves back and forth between two extreme areas. These areas I call the limitation of the range:

Upper limit (upper horizontal line): resistance

Lower limit (lower horizontal line): support

However, we can only identify a range when the market touches at least twice the resistance and the support.

Image 4, US T-Note 10 Future, hourly chart, July 19–21, 2017

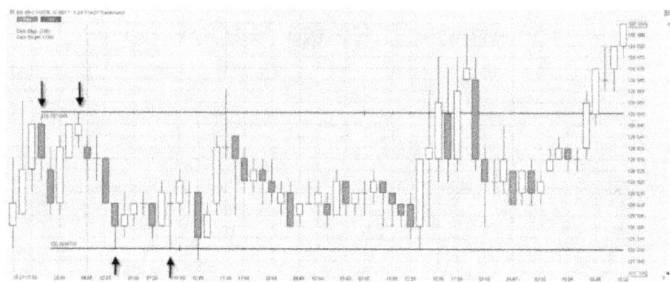

Image 4 shows a screenshot of the T-Note Futures, the American Futures on the ten-year bonds. On the left in the chart, I marked the first two touches up and down with an arrow. After the second touch had taken place at the support, the range existed. In general, the more points of contact with the support line or line of resistance happen, the more significant (or stronger) the range becomes.

In addition, it becomes more difficult to dissolve the range. In other words, it takes a kind of catalyst (important economic news or a lot of money) in order for a breakout of the range to succeed. This happened in the above example at the resistance (white candles on the far right of the chart). However, there was a first attempt the day before, which failed. After a few hours, the market fell back into the range. The range had therefore continued. I would like to discuss how to deal with such a scenario.

One could also say that the market is caught between a support level (where buyers are more likely to appear) and a resistance level (where more sellers emerge). The markets then jump back and forth between the two areas like a ping-pong ball.

Just as a range, once identified, begins, it will end one day. This happens by a breakout from the range. As already said: there may be several failed attempts for a breakout of the range. At some point, a breakout will succeed, and then the range is over.

I do not know of any method to predict the end of a range, just as I cannot predict the future of a market. All I can say is that the trader one day realizes that a breakout from the range has succeeded and that the market does not return to the range.

However, the attentive trader must also realize that markets resume once- abandoned ranges after some time. I will show some examples of this.

The basic idea of range trading is to open buy positions in the area of support and close them as soon as the market reaches the upper limit of the range. Conversely, traders can open up short positions and close them as soon as the market reaches the support line.

The trader can repeat this strategy as long as the market stays within the trading range.

The advantages of this approach are obvious:

- There is an unlimited number of trading ranges at all times and in all financial markets.

- Range trading clearly defines the entry point and the exit point (buy or sell): upper or lower limit of the range.

- The price target is always the other side of the range: for long positions, the upper limit; for short positions, the lower limit.

- Range trading clearly defines the risk/reward ratio. The trader knows exactly how much he can win with the trade. If the other side is 100 points from the entry, the maximum profit is 100 points.

- Thus, Range trading defines the risk very clear too. If the trader can win 100 points and wants to work with a risk/reward ratio of 1:2, his stop must be 50 points below the buy entry.

- Range trading often has a hit rate higher than 50%. The trader can thus also choose a "poorer" risk/reward ratio and still operate profitably.

A poorer risk/reward ratio can mean that he risks exactly as many points as he wants to achieve. In the example above, he could decide to put the stop 100 points away from the entry, even if he has only a 100-point goal. In this case, the trader works with a 1:1 risk/reward ratio. He would need at least a 51% hit rate to trade profitably (before commissions).

I do not criticize that. There may be good reasons why a trader opts for such a model. The advantage is obvious: the market will hit his stop less often. If he loses, however, he loses twice as much as in the 1:2 model.

We should not overlook the fact, however, that range trading strategies, like any other strategy, involve **disadvantages**:

- Range trading limits the profit initially by the clearly defined price target.

- Markets do not always adhere to existing range limits.

- Breakouts from the range, which take place opposite the position of the trader, lead to losses.

- The market does not always hit the price target, which of course reduces the overall profit.

- Traders cannot always clearly identify the range.

I will discuss all these points go into detail on how to identify a range. In addition, I will focus on the problem of the false breakout from ranges using several examples. In addition, I will go into detail on the issue of the risk/reward ratio, which also plays an important role in range trading. Finally, a large part of the trading success results from the right combination of reward, risk, and trading opportunities. I will also discuss why traders can use this formula excellently in range trading.

3. Look to the left!

In conversations with traders, when looking at charts, I noticed repeatedly how few of them <u>look to the left</u>. What do I mean by that?

On a financial chart, the time line always runs from left to right (in China, I have been told it should be the other way around, but this is, of course, a trader joke!). Therefore, if we want to know what happened in the past, we should look to the left.

Of course, despite the clear price trend on the left side of the chart, we cannot predict the future price trend, as desirable as this might be. Nevertheless, there is something like a **market memory**. This means that the market players seem to "remember" striking price levels (mostly highs and lows) of the past few days. By "remember," I mean only that as soon as the market comes back to such a level, market participants perceive such a level as more or less significant. No wonder, because these levels are pretty much the only tangible thing in the middle of a chaos of data that seem to run directionless across the screen.

For example, if the EUR/USD on the previous day made a high at 1.1420, you can expect that the market players remember this as soon as the market reaches the same level again. The question remains unspoken: Will the market turn down here again? Alternatively, do we go beyond this level today? The same applies, of course, to the lows.

Such levels may stay significant for several days, and even weeks. In some cases, the market "remembers" important turning points that have occurred months earlier. This was certainly the case when this level happened with major market decisions, such as interest rate decisions of a central bank, political elections, or other decisions, which can fundamentally change the perception of a market. The trader should pay attention to such levels. Markets do not simply go over such a level.

The difficulty in drawing horizontal lines in the chart, which make these levels visible, is, of course, in the interpretation of what is important and what is not. Sometimes the trader has to make corrections because the price action seems to take a different level more important than the trader initially favored. There is no shame in drawing a line on the chart, which has no consequences, while another level you have overlooked is constantly touched.

Even though I have been doing this for years, I am wrong now and then and must make corrections. Again, Mr. Market likes to play with the expectations of the participants. One should say goodbye to the idea that this is an exact science.

Image 5: EUR/USD, 4-hour chart, June 12 to July 12, 2017

As an example of the importance of "look to the left," we may apply a section from the June 2017 EUR/USD. The arrows indicate price levels at which the market recalls significant highs or lows of the past few days. In some cases, the market even turned at exactly the same price as soon as it reached the old price level. In other cases, it exaggerates a bit and then rows back.

In other words, markets like to build up in such a way that, before they go on, they like to return first to old price levels, which they already conquered in the past. Such pullbacks-skilled traders can trade, but this is not the subject of the book.

Of course, you can trade without this knowledge. However, if you are going to deal with range trading, "look to the left!" should become one of your maxims. For often, you will find something on the left side of the chart to which the present trading of the market relates. Is this not valuable information?

Now, "look to the left" is not a magic formula that will only give you profits on the stock exchange. This method will help you to better identify the current "playing field."

This is especially important for range trading, because once you are able to identify the limits of the playing field, you may have found the entry and exit points of your future trades. Range trading is very simple. However, to make it easy, you should first see the left side of the chart clearly.

Once you have learned to pay attention to these significant points, you have at least the chance to assess the current market situation in a better way.

You may still be unable to predict it – no one can – but you can formulate a realistic estimate of where the future price evolution might go. If you can make the right decision in more than 50% of the cases, you might be able to build a profitable trading business.

For you to be able to do so, we should first consider how to draw horizontal support and resistance lines correctly.

4. How Do I Draw Proper Support and Resistance Lines?

There seems to be real confusion and false ideas in the trader community about how to draw horizontal support and resistance lines correctly. I will try to clear up some misunderstandings.

Now, in the previous chapter "Look to the left," I worked out the importance of significant swing highs or swing lows. In any case, the trader should include these levels in his considerations.

The practice shows, however, that "the market" does not always respect such levels 100%. If the trader rates a price level as significant, this means that many contracts will change owners around this level. That means many traders will close positions or change from short to long and vice versa.

One can therefore speak of **support zones** and **resistance zones** rather than support lines or resistance lines. An example from the Eurostoxx50 Future (FESX) may illustrate this.

Image 6: FESX, hourly chart, November 10, 2016 to December 6, 2016

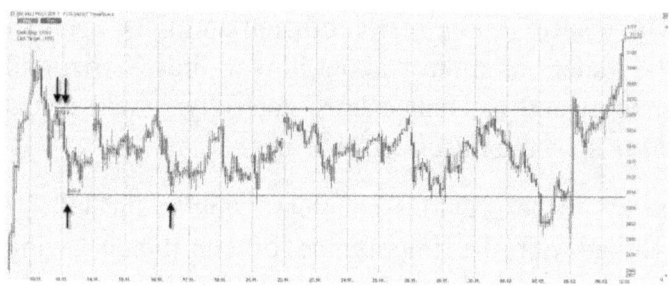

In this example in the Eurostoxx future, I drew the two lines "super correct." That is, I have linked the top of the two highs of the range (at 3062 points) and the two lows (at 3007 points). At first sight, this image looks very neat. I have covered the range quite well. Looking more closely, however, one can see that many turning points have not touched the line. This is both the case at the support and certainly at the resistance.

The market seemed to have a somewhat different view where these levels were over time, as I had assumed with my hypercorrect representation. That is why it is not wrong at all if you adjust your lines over time to the real turning points of the market. You should not expect the market to always respect your levels, which they don't do anyway. That is why I have adapted my lines somewhat. The result looks as follows:

Image 7: FESX, hourly chart, Nov 10, 2016 to Dec 6, 2016, second attempt

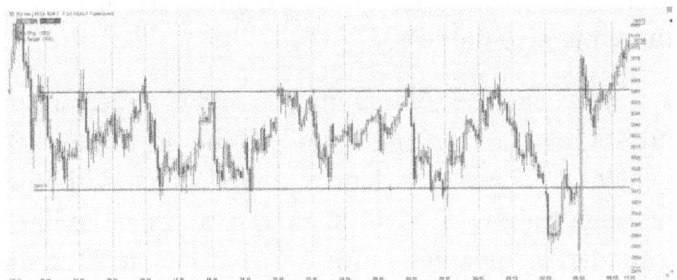

You see in this adjustment of the lines that the range has become somewhat narrower. The resistance line is now at 3055 and the support line is at 3011 points. I even made the sacrilege to draw my line through several shadows and even the body of some of the candles.

The fact is, however, that in this representation many more turning points have come about than in the first representation. Alone at the support, there are now 13(!) turning points. It therefore speaks for itself that for the market, the level 3011 apparently was more significant with the time than the first low at 3007 (low of 11.11.2017).

Now the difference between 3007 and 3011 is not huge, and that is the reason why I speak here of support zones. In this area, there were an increasing number of buyers as sellers in this period, which is why the market here has mostly turned up again. Because this happened more and more with 3011 than with 3006, I then also adapted the line. Not more but also not less.

As you can see, drawing "correct" lines is a question of a reasonable understanding of market behavior. There was hardly any contact with the resistance above at my first attempt to draw the line. The market apparently turned earlier, not at 3062, as initially assumed, but already at 3055. If you do not take note of this as a trader, you will never come to a trade.

5. In Which Markets Can You Operate Range Trading?

Answer: in all.

There are, of course, certain risks that the trader should know before he starts. Gaps, for example, are an issue in all markets. They always arise as soon as a market closes at any time and reopens the next day (or next Monday after a weekend).

As a rule, the gaps are small and will have little effect on the outcome of the current trade. There are, however, occasional bigger gaps. They can occur in favor of the trader or to his disadvantage. External catalysts (terrorist attacks, earthquakes, and unexpected exits of elections or surveys such as the Brexit) sometimes trigger extreme events on the stock market. They are very difficult or almost impossible to predict.

In more recent times, such events also occur without a known catalyst. This was the case, for example, with the so-called "flash crash" of May 6, 2010, when the SP500 and the Dow Jones Index rushed almost 10% within minutes. I still remember the day very well, because I had a small, short position in the EUR/JPY. I could hardly believe my eyes when I realized that my position stood at a blow over 900 pips in the win. I was lucky that day. I was, so to speak, on the right side of the action.

If I had a long position in the EUR/JPY, my stop would have been touched. The execution of my order would probably have been worse because of the extreme volatility, but my position would be out of the market before it could lead to a major loss.

Currencies

Therefore, if you do not like gaps or do not want other extreme events to affect your trading, I recommend exclusive range trading with currencies. Forex markets are open 24 hours, which means there are no overnight gaps to fear. Traders should close their positions before the weekend to eliminate the risk of weekend gaps. In addition, you can reopen the trade on Sunday evening or Monday morning easily, should your scenario still be valid. Many traders do just that.

*Stocks

The advantage of range trading in equities is that trading ranges can last long. Traders can therefore trade them very profitably. If an investor starts selling repeatedly, as soon as a share reaches a certain price level, his behavior will establish a resistance zone. A wise range trader can benefit from this opportunity.

You can also observe this phenomenon at the bottom of the range. Sometimes a big buyer "catches" a stock at a certain price. This creates a support zone. Such levels may last for weeks until "the buyer" ceases to buy and the stock starts to rise or fall.

Disadvantages of stocks are the overnight gaps, which can sometimes turn out to be extreme. They are often much larger than in the other markets. Once I had a long position in the shares of the German software manufacturer SAP. Before the market opening, news came out of a sales slump in the USA. As a result, the stock opened more than eight percent lower. I had to take a huge loss, and unfortunately, no stop-loss orders help with overnight gaps.

This incident was the main reason I stopped trading stocks. Nevertheless, as I said, this is my decision. In the longer term, the impact of such extreme events is balanced. It is up to the trader to decide whether to accept such outliers (in his favor or disadvantage).

I have decided that stocks are not good instruments for short-term trading, even if they can be very profitable on occasion. I prefer to trade liquid futures markets whose overnight gaps rarely exceed 1%.

Futures

Most professional traders I know trade futures. There is a good reason for this. Futures are very fair and liquid financial instruments. In other words, the trader generally gets a fair and good execution. This applies to both the entry and the exit, and for stop-loss orders. Phenomena such as slippage (you get a worse execution price than intended) occur here rather rarely, if at all, and only on very volatile days.

For this reason, for example, index futures such as the E-Mini, Mini-Dow, FDAX, or Nikkei 225 Future are good trading vehicles to implement a range trading strategy. However, I strongly recommend that the trader keep an eye on the economic calendar. Markets can become very volatile, especially when central banks publish interest rate decisions.

You can also operate range trading with bond futures and commodity futures. However, here too, the trader should pay attention when expecting important news. In the case of commodities in particular, a sudden rise of volatility can occur, especially if the commodity future has been trading in a range for a long time. It is often wiser to close the position before traders expect some important news or an economic report.

6. How to Trade a Range in Practice

In Chapter 4, I discussed how you can identify a horizontal range on the chart at all. It is not always easy to answer this question because in some cases, the scope for interpretation remains open. It depends then ultimately on the trader's skills (or experience) whether he actually recognizes a range as such or not.

Financial markets are and remain chaotic structures, and no one will ever be able to say with certainty what is going on now. In the background, as is well known, all kind of things are going on, and unexpected events (economic news, central bank decisions) can poke just "support" and "resistance" in seconds, as if they had never existed.

Therefore, the trader should always be aware of this fact, especially when something appears so obvious on the chart that it feels like a direct invitation to trade. The trader should thus always work with stop loss orders in order to protect the account from oversized losses.

It must be clear to every trader that no matter what he sees or thinks he sees on a chart, his view is ultimately an interpretation of reality. Whoever draws a line in a chart does not have the authority to say: "up here and no further!"

As every experienced trader knows, prices can always go higher (or lower), even if it seems absurd. The best example is the current bull market (as of September 2017) in the American stock indices. For months (years), crash prophets prophesied the "end" of this bull market. Well, at some point this bull market will eventually come to an end, no question. Nevertheless, it could be that this bull market lasts much longer than the crash prophets want to hold true. There are enough historical examples for this.

Traders therefore live only from the grace of probability. The likelihood is higher that the market will turn again at this point because of previous pivot points. It does not have to, but the data in the chart indicate an increased probability. Although it does not have to be so this time, those who repeatedly observe this scenario might find that this to be true in most cases (50% + ...).

A trader is therefore a person who repeatedly takes calculated risks, which he knows carry a (small) statistical advantage. This statistical advantage is the one, which, after a series of trades, will account for the difference between profit and loss. That is what trading is all about.

As far as range trading is concerned, this is precisely the case. A range trader is someone who, based on observation, assumes that market players will respect the upper and lower limits of the range (until the day of the successful breakout from the range).

If the range trader proceeds from this assumption, it makes sense to closely observe the events at the limits of the range in the hope of finding indications that confirm or reinforce this assumption. Since in the above examples some of the signals on the hourly chart were not confirmed, the trader should switch the chart to a lower timeframe.

For example, if a market in the hourly chart touches a line of resistance, it makes sense to look at the 30-minute chart or the 15-minute chart to find tradable evidence that justifies a trade. It is therefore imperative that the trader waits for a clearly **recognizable signal** before placing the limit order.

By *signal,* I mean that the market should indicate that it intends to respect the resistance or the support. Occasionally, the market will, for example, touch the support exactly and then immediately turn up again. This would be a signal, but as the market hardly touches the support, the trader does not have time to consider a trade. Traders should not jump on the moving train here, because in range trading, it is all about calmly entering calculated trades.

If the market breaks the support and stays there for several hours, this is not a signal either. Only when the market recaptures the support after a few hours does the trader get a trading signal. Because it shows him that the sellers have tried to push the market down, but obviously they failed. This fact would justify for me a buy position with price target resistance. In order to show such a signal even more clearly, we look more closely at an example in the EUR/JPY.

Image 8: EUR/JPY, hourly chart, June 11 to June 13, 2017

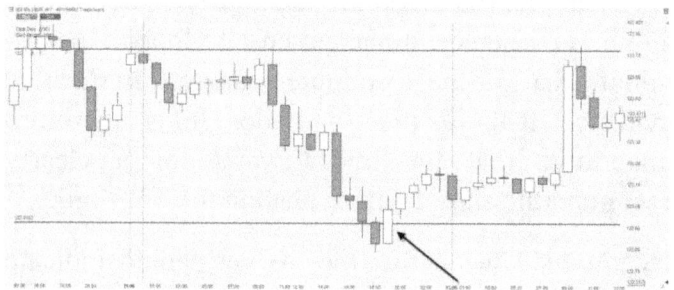

In this example, in the EU/JPY hourly chart, the aforementioned scenario occurred. The currency pair approaches the support and falls short of it (red candle below the horizontal line below). The next candle is then again bullish and has a closing price above the support line (arrow below). The buyers took control of the market again. The market thus confirmed the existence of the range.

Because the trader cannot buy after the end of the bullish hour candle for reasons of risk management (because then he would have to buy some pips over the support), he must observe the market behavior at a lower time level.

You could criticize this approach because the trader leaves the observed time level (hourly chart) and looks for the signal at a lower time level. However, if you do not do this, you would lose too many trades.

The trader should nevertheless be aware that the lower he chooses the time level, the less significant the signals become. In summary, I can recommend the following approach:

Signal chart	**Entry chart**
Daily chart:	4-hour chart, hourly chart
4-hour chart:	Hourly chart, 30-minute chart
Hourly chart:	30-minute chart, 15-minute chart

It makes no sense to me, for example, when the trader identifies a signal on a 4-hour chart, then looks for an entry on the 5-minute chart. He should therefore look for an entry on the next lower level, i.e., on the hourly chart or on the 30-minute chart.

Image 9: EUR/JPY, 15-minutes chart, June 12, 2017

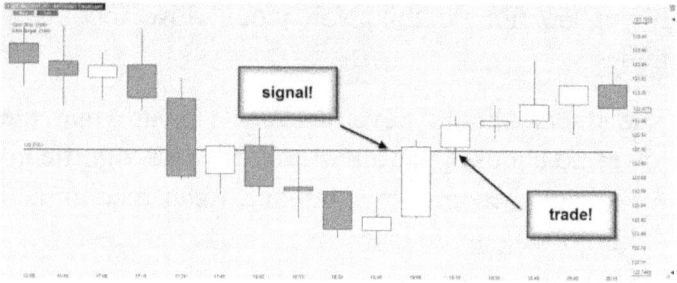

I could identify the above-mentioned example in the EUR/JPY in the 15-minute chart. You can see the pair lingering under the support line after the break of the support (left in the chart). Then a white candle conquered the line again (Signal!). Only then, we have a clear signal. After the close of this candle, the trader can place a limited buy order on the support line.

My entry criteria for range trading are therefore relatively strict. The reason is simple. Since a range only includes a restricted price target (and thus a limited profit potential), I do not want to reduce that potential profit by buying some points or pips over the limit, because some candle on a chart closed somewhat higher.

For reasons of risk management, I place my trade exactly at the price where the support line runs. I want to have this price and no other. If the trader operates in this way, he shows that he intends <u>to play according to his rules</u> and not according to what the market is doing right now.

In the example above, the next candle on the 15-minute chart then only briefly fell below the support line, which usually means that the order was executed. The trader now has a long position.

If the market had not touched the support line and would have risen straight up, it would not have executed the order. This happened, for example, in the next example.

Image 10: EUR/JPY, 15-Minute chart, June 13, 2017

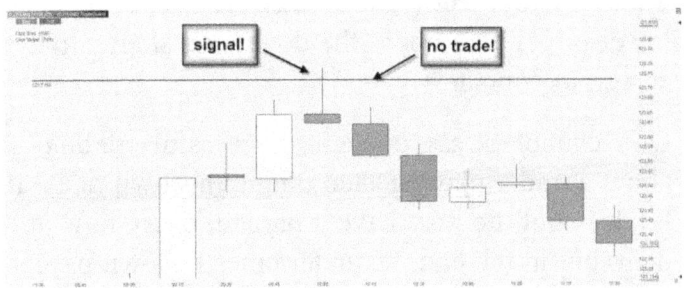

In this example, the market reached the upper limit of the range. At the same time, the price dropped back into the range and thus triggered a short signal on the 15-minute chart. The trader could place a limited sell order on the line of resistance (horizontal line above).

Unfortunately, the market did not execute this order. The next candle opened some pips under the resistance line and closed deeper without touching the resistance line again: no trade!

The market then steered back into the support line of the range. This was, of course, "annoying" because the EUR/JPY reached its price target the day after. It "would" have been a profitable trade, if the trader had taken this trade. "Had" and "would" are verbs that a trader should remove from his vocabulary. As Image 10 shows, the conditions for the trade were fulfilled, but the order was not executed.

I know that some traders would have taken this trade anyway. They would then have had to pay a lower price. This opens the door for a sloppy trader career, of course.

One cannot stress enough: Successful trading is about a trader playing according to his own rules. If he does not, he may have a bargain every now and then, but in the end, he undermines his own psyche by making the market determine his own actions.

I hope the reader sees the fundamental difference! Either the market drives the trader like a ship without a captain or he determines himself how and when he enters the market and under what conditions.

This, of course, requires a certain degree of rigidity, which must be appropriated so that one learns to accept giving away such seeming opportunities. Sometimes the market gives you pips and sometimes it takes your pips. As a trader, you do not have control over this. What you can control are the conditions in which you are willing to act or not. If you find the conditions fulfilled, then act. If they are not, keep your hands still.

It is, however, easy to give this recommendation. I know from my own experience how quickly I am inclined to run behind an apparent chance. If you do it once, this is by no means a broken leg. However, if do this time and time again, it becomes a (bad) habit. Eventually, this habit will lead to bad results. Ultimately, those people are then blaming financial markets, saying trading does not work. Unfortunately, the cemetery of failed traders is quite large, and if I can only keep one trader from doing this impulsively, I did not write this book in vain.

Limited orders are very important, especially in range trading, because every point and every pip counts. If the trader enters the market with a market order out of fear that he might miss a trade, he will usually get a worse price. What real businessperson acts in such a way? However, since the order is only one click away when trading, there is always a danger that traders will trade impulsively and accept lower prices.

I have a friend who has a trading company in fruit juices. I once asked him what a truck with strawberries would cost when he gave up this order. The answer was about 8,000 euros. Do you seriously believe that my friend does not care if he sends a truck with strawberries across Europe, whether the price is 8,100 or 7,950? I can tell you, it does matter to him. He will save every euro he can save; otherwise, he will not buy the strawberries.

I believe this commercial attitude is one a trader should also have. Trading with limited orders means: this is the price I am willing to pay; otherwise, I will not buy!

With this "avaricious mindset," you will miss a good trade every now and then. This is self-explanatory. However, do not forget: you make the profit when buying. So be very stingy.

Image 11: Corn Future, 4-hour chart, March 16 to June 7, 2017

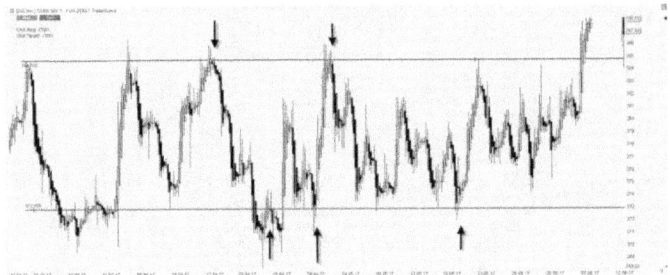

Sometimes it is worth looking beyond the traditional trading markets and having a look at "unconventional markets" like commodities. I found a nice trading range in the corn future from March to June 2017. Commodity markets tend to stay longer in a trading range. If no relevant news changes the fundamental view of the main market players, there is no reason for trends.

In this case, corn oscillated for three months between $384 and $372. Not much at first sight but sufficient for a futures trader. After the range became visible (I had to make several corrections on the lines), I detected four signals, which all hit their targets. In this case, I used the heikin ashi representation of the chart.

Image 12: Corn Future, hourly chart, March 16 to June 7, 2017

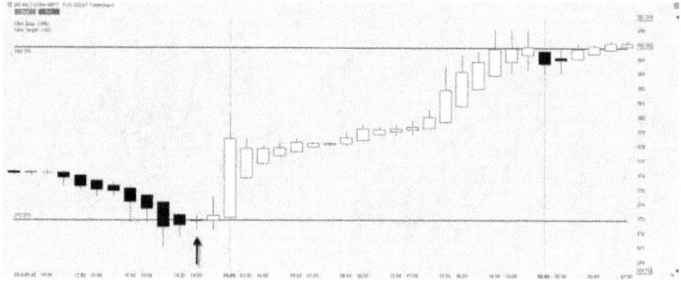

When I switched to the shorter hourly chart, I found an interesting situation at the support. We see a downward wave (black candles on the left), which led to a short undercut of the support line. After another candle that did not make a new low, the market drew a doji exactly at the support line (arrow below).

Image 13: Dojis and Spinning Tops

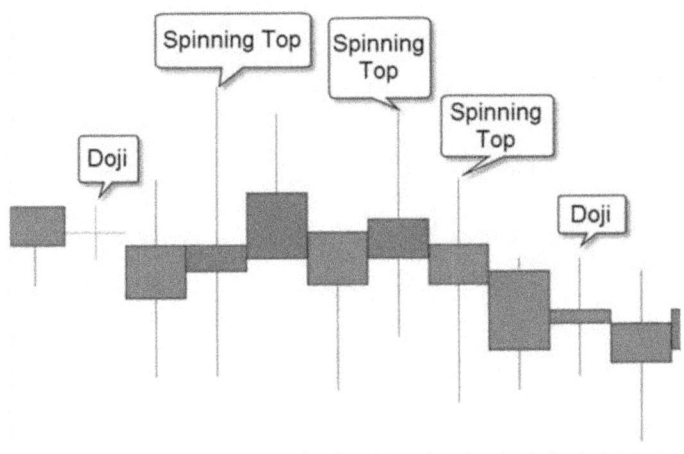

Image 13 shows some dojis and spinning tops. Dojis have no or only a very small body with small shadows. A Doji often looks like a plus sign. Spinning tops have long shadows above or below the core body. Both patterns illustrate uncertainty in the market. Neither bears nor bulls currently dominate the market.

A doji (as in Image 12 of the corn futures) always symbolizes a kind of balance between buyers and sellers. On the one hand, the sellers had driven the market to the support zone. There it briefly undercut the zone. Then the market did not make any new lows anymore and finally at the support, a doji emerged. For me, this is a good reason to put a buy order with target resistance line. The next trading day confirmed this assessment (on May 1, 2017).

7. Where Should I Place the Stop?

Any serious trading strategy must address the question of risk. This is also the case with range trading. A not to be underestimated advantage of range trading is the fact that the stop does not have to be set according to chart technical criteria.

The reason is simple: the upper and lower limits mark the range exactly. We have to consider everything that happens above or below the range as a chart-technical "new ground" that does not belong to the playing field of the range.

Therefore, I recommend placing the stop according to risk management criteria and not according to certain patterns in the chart. For example, if you are ready to risk as much as you can win, you can simply calculate the stop distance to the entry price based on the width of the range.

If the range is, for example, 100 points wide, the trader can put the stop 100 points below the entry price (or 100 points above the entry for a short position).

Since this trader risks as much as he can win, he needs a hit rate of at least 51% to be profitable.

Trader A: RRR = 1:1

51 winning trades x 100 = 5100 points

49 losing trades x 100 =   4900 points

Net total: 200 points

Trader A, who has a 1:1 risk/reward ratio (RRR), needs a good hit rate. It must be over 50% if he wants to make money.

There are, however, traders who prefer to set the profits in proportion to a number of losses. These traders especially want to win more when they win, and lose less when they lose. They choose, for example, a risk/reward ratio (RRR) of 1:2. This trader will want to realize a profit of 100 points at a range of 100 points wide. However, his stop is only 50% of the range. He will put it 50 points away from the entry price. In this case, the calculation would look as follows:

Trader B: RRR = 1: 2

34 winning trades x 100 = 3400 points

66 losing trades x 50 =   3300 points

Net total: 100 points

Trader B is thus in the comfortable position that he only needs to be "right" at 34% of his trades to be profitable. The disadvantage of his method is, of course, that the market will hit the stop more often than in Trader As system, which has his stop farther away from the entry price.

Of course, besides these two risk management models, countless variants exist. I know, for example, an oil trader who even works with negative risk/reward ratios. His stop is really far from the current market, usually 200 cents or more. His price targets are smaller, however, usually at 20 or 30 cents. The market rarely hits his stop, and he usually closes the trade when he realizes that the trade is going in the wrong direction. He has a kind of internal "time-stop," while his actual stop is only a kind of "disaster stop."

I do not recommend following him. It works for him, but I am sure that many traders would not feel comfortable with this kind of risk management.

Depending on the risk model, there are different ways to change the parameters so that the trader can optimize the result. Trader A, who works with an RRR of 1:1, will not be able to change much on his hit rate because it is already high (over 50%). However, like the oil trader, he can try to close his losing trades faster and not let them hit the stop.

If, for example, he was able to lose an average of only 70 points instead of 100, then his net result would be much better.

Trader A: RRR = 0.7:1

51 winning trades x 100 = 5100 points

49 Losing trades x 70 =   3430 points

Net total: 1670 points

In this case, Trader A could expect a net profit of 1670 points or 16.70 points per trade after 100 trades. That sounds much better than the mingy 2 points per trade, which he made initially (if he lets the losing trades being stopped out consistently at 100 points and not earlier).

In addition, trader B can optimize his result. Since he already works with a clearly narrower stop loss as Trader A, the optimization options are lower (although they do exist). Trader B could try to achieve a better hit rate through a qualitative selection of his trades. He could try to reach a hit rate of 50% instead of a hit rate of just 34%. If this were the case, the results would look like this:

Trader B: RRR = 1:2

50 winning trades x 100 = 5000 points

50 losing trades x 50 =   2500 points

Net total: 2500 points

In this case, Trader B would even be able to expect a net profit of 2500 points or 25 points per trade after 100 trades. This is an even better result than that of the optimized system of Trader A.

Of course, these examples are purely hypothetical and the struggle for profitability often proves to be harder in real trading than it can appear here. When I say that Trader B can obtain such a result, it will only happen if he actually improves the quality of his trades. In this book, it will also be a matter of finding the best possible entries in the knowledge that there will always be losing trades. Whenever you consider a new trading strategy like range trading, you should always calculate with a realistic picture of the amount of winning AND losing trades.

8. Questions of Trade Management

A. Should You Close the Trade Before the Weekend?

If the trader has efficiently identified the entry point, the exit point (target), and the stop loss level, the question remains as to how to "manage" a current trade as long as neither the price target nor the stop has been reached. This question arises especially before the weekend (elections) and before important events on the stock market (interest rate decisions of central banks).

If you prefer to be "flat" on the weekend, I definitely recommend closing all current trades, whether they are in profit or in the loss. The same applies, of course, to the interest rate decisions of central banks. These are not always as dramatic as one would expect. Here, I recommend staying in the trade, especially if you operate in higher periods such as the hourly chart or even four-hour chart or daily chart. Do not let yourself be influenced too much by such events. Sometimes the result will be to your advantage, sometimes to your disadvantage. More important is the consistency of your trade decisions and how good your risk management is.

On the weekends you risk being surprised by a gap that surpasses your risk stop on Monday or Sunday evening for Forex traders (the opposite happens too:

a Monday gap that by far surpasses your price target).

In my experience, markets balance out profits and losses at such events in the longer term. That is why you should tackle the matter calmly. Only those traders should be afraid of gaps that are operating with too much leverage in the markets (traders who operate with too large positions). These traders should not be on the stock market. The faster markets throw them out, the shorter the pain.

B. Should You Use Trailing Stops When Range Trading?

A trailing stop is a wonderful tool that traders can use to maximize profits. This is especially important when the trader already has a position with a high profit and wants to pull the last tics or pips out of the trade. Here a trailing stop can certainly be helpful.

However, if you are range trading, the price target is limited. Within the range, the strangest things can happen. It is a completely different market situation than when the trader has a position in a long-lasting trend, which now ends and from which he wants to take the very last points.

That is why I advise not to use a trailing stop for range or channel trading. As a rule, you will not be able to optimize your profits. Trailing stops use to get you out of the trade before your position hits the target.

In range trading, I trust support and resistance. Sometimes short spikes (outliers) happen in one direction or the other. If you then have a take-profit at the other range limit, you can be put out of the trade faster than you ever hoped. These are the little gifts for range traders. These taste very sweet!

C. What Should You Do if the Trade Goes "nowhere"?

This situation occurs quite often. You have a position; the trade is in the middle of the range (it is profitable) but the market has hardly moved for hours (or days). When the weekend approaches, you can close the trade.

If you feel insecure, I always recommend either closing or at least reducing the position. For example, if you have two contracts, you can close one and wait to see if the desired scenario might happen for the second contract. If this still does not happen after a certain time, I recommend closing the second contract as well.

D. Should I Push the Stop Closer to the Market?

Here I would be very careful. As I said, within the range, strange things happen. You will see that, for example, a long position has almost hit the price target (the line of resistance), and suddenly the price springs back to the support as if it had to take another run-up to finally hit the upper limit of the range. This scenario occurs quite often.

For this reason, in range trading, I would never place the stop within the range.

You can put the stop slightly closer to the entry level to minimize the risk if the trade is close to the price target. However, as I said, I am rather cautious and do not believe that such measures have a positive influence on your results (from the point of view of hundreds or thousands of trades).

More important to me is that the trader learns to trust his system. This will have a positive impact on the results in the medium term. When a trader trusts his system, he also takes positions that many of his competitors would not take. These are often the most profitable. In addition, this is what distinguishes a professional from an amateur. A professional sees a signal, takes the trade without any ifs and buts, precisely because he knows his system, and insists on its statistical advantage.

Whoever manipulates his stop too much suggests to his subconscious: I do not trust this position.

In a longer term (from a thousand trades upward), this plays hardly a role. Sometimes you might have a smaller loss when putting the stop closer, when the trade is going against you, but eventually it will reach the target anyway.

Rather, the quality of the trades taken and their consistent execution will optimize the results. A chosen risk/reward ratio of at least 1:2 will eventually work to the advantage of the trader. Provided the hit rate is above 33.33%.

However, these are very pessimistic hit rates. Realistic hit rates for range trading tend to be in the range of 50–60%. Even at a meager hit rate of 40 or 45%, range trading can be very profitable, if the trader does not manipulate the risk/reward ratio too much. Say he allows the market to decide whether the market hits the take profit order or the stop.

9. Examples of Range Markets

A. Trading Ranges in the Foreign Exchange Market

Image 14: EUR/JPY, hourly chart, June 6 to June 16, 2017

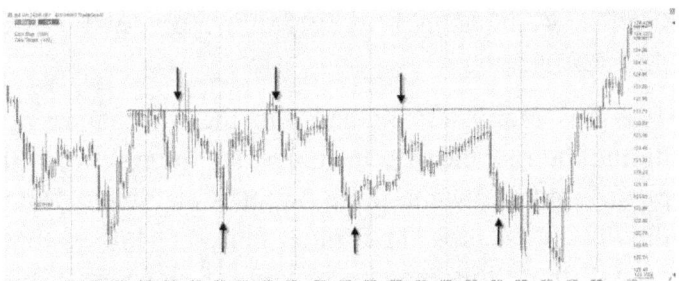

A trading range is not always easy to identify. It is important, as already stated, that there are at least two touches with the support line and with the resistance line. Only then can we talk about a range as in the above example in the hourly chart of the EUR/JPY. Only after the trader had discovered the range could he determine trading signals (arrows in the chart) that relate to the range.

In the above example in the EUR/JPY, there were six trading signals: three short signals (arrows on the top) and three long signals (arrows below). The range was set between 123.71 and 122.91 and thus had a fluctuation of 80 pips. This is sufficient so that a reasonable risk management is possible. If the trader chooses a 1:2 risk/reward ratio, the trader will place the stop loss order 40 pips away from the entry price.

For the trader to realize the profit as soon as the market hits the target of the trade, I always recommend using **bracket orders** for range trading. This means that the trader can accompany the position at the same time by a stop-loss order and a take-profit order.

This has many advantages. On the one hand, we define the risk clearly. In Image 14, the risk was 40 pips. In addition, the price target is also clear from the outset: 80 pips. The trader therefore knows that he will trade this range profitably if he scores a hit of over 33.33%. In other words, 60% of the trades can end in a loss; the outcome would still be a profit, albeit a small profit.

Such clear and unambiguous presettings are invaluable if you want to build a viable long-term business. Good traders always work with crystal-clear parameters, which they can accurately describe at any time. This is also why I am a fan of range trading because here I am the master of the game.

In addition, you do not need to babysit your trades, at least as long as you work in time frames of an hour or higher. Most of these trades will take several hours to a few days until they reach their price target. That is why we look at the six trades in the EUR/JPY in Image 14 somewhat more closely.

Trade 1: Short 123.71: Here the market came close to the stop but did not hit it. The market hit the take profit order the next day.

Trade 2: Long 122.91: The trade never came into the problems. The market hit the take profit order in the evening that day.

Trade 3: Short 123.71: The market hit the profit order the evening of the next day.

Trade 4: Long 122.91: The market hit the profit order the next day.

Trade 5: Short 123.91: The market hit the profit order after two days.

Trade 6: Long 122.91: The market closed the trade the next day with a 40 pips loss.

The results of these six trades:

5 winning trades x 80 pips = 400 pips

<u>1 losing trade x 40 pips =   40 pips</u>

Net total: 360 pips

It is also interesting to note that the loss trade happened by a fake breakout that came before the actual breakout. Anyone who recognized this could have traded it, but this is a somewhat more advanced level, which I will deal with a later.

It is important first that you recognize the advantages of the range trading strategy. It is a very unspectacular strategy, but it can be very successful if the trader carries it out consistently.

Now, as a range trader, you will not always be able to achieve such excellent results as with these six trades in the EUR/JPY. For example, all profit trades hit the price target, but this is not always the case. In this case, the trader could exploit the maximum potential. If one or two of his trades fail to hit the price target or only half, the results will clearly be less glamorous.

In addition, on these six trades, there was only one loss. This corresponds to a hit rate of 83.33%, which is, of course, excellent. The trader will not always achieve such a score. However, even hit rates of 50% are usually sufficient to build a profitable business with this method.

The basis of this business is:

1. The observation of a basket of tradable markets

2. A clear setup based on support and resistance

3. A realistic risk/reward ratio

A trader can do this without permanently "monitoring" his trades. A working time of one to two hours a day should be enough.

Image 15: GBP/JPY, 2-hour chart February 26 to March 23, 2017

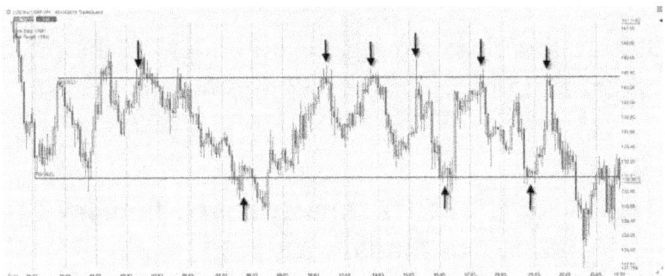

Another range, which I had made up in the GBP/JPY pair, generated nine signals, six on the short side and three on the long side. The upper limit of the range I had set at 140.35. The lower limit was 139.00. The fluctuation margin of this range was therefore 135 pips, which you can expect in the case of a currency pair such as the GBP/JPY.

If the trader assumes the same risk/reward ratio as in the EUR/JPY, his price target would be 135 pips and his risk equals 67 pips. Interestingly, there was no loss in this example. There were some false breakouts that initially ran counter to the trade, but even the first long position (arrow left below), which had been in the loss for two days, finally hit its target.

However, two short trades did not hit the target (the second and third arrows on the upper left). They returned to the resistance line without causing losses. I would therefore consider these trades as breakeven trades. Result = zero.

Despite this shortcoming, seven trades hit the price target of 135 pips. That is 935 pips in four weeks!

Image 16: USD/CHF, hourly chart, January 22 to January 31, 2017

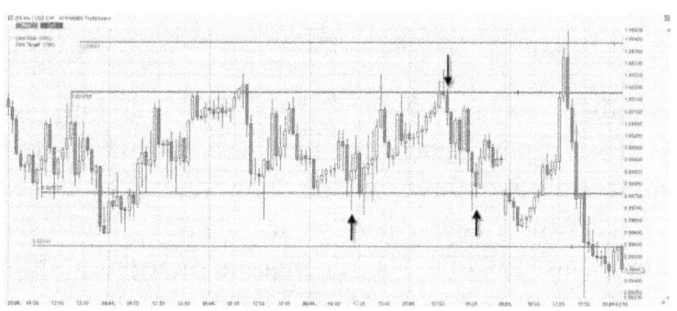

I found a modest range at the end of January 2017 in the USD/CHF pair. The upper limit was 1.0018. The lower limit was 0.9972. In other words, the pair in this period traded by the currency parity (1,000). Ranges at such striking levels quite often occur. Here, the lots gladly change the owners, which this range vividly demonstrates. For a shrewd range trader, there is an opportunity here and there to collect some pips in the wind shadow of the big players.

In total, there were three valid trading signals (arrows) during this period of nine days, all of which were profitable. The range was only 44 pips wide. That means the stop stood 21 pips away from the entry. The two red lines above and below mark the stop placements of the trades. The market never hit them.

After the second long signal was bought (the arrow at the bottom right), the pair opened after the weekend with a small down-gap, but the position was never in danger. A few hours later, the market hit the take profit order.

B. Deeper Examination of a Sideways Period in the E-Mini

Image 17: E-mini, 4-hour heikin ashi chart, May 22 to July 11, 2017

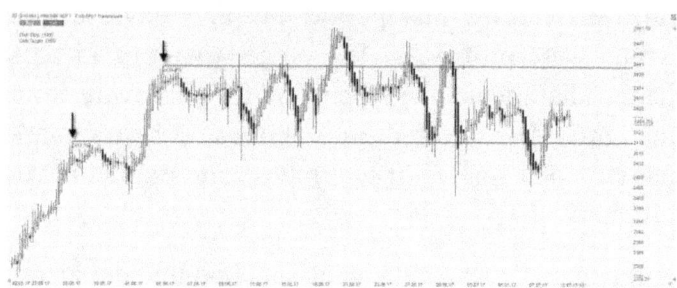

Between the end of May and the end of July 2017, the American index SP500 moved into a sideways phase, which I will take a closer look at. The two arrows, which marked two significant highs at the previous rally (left in the chart), proved later to be the two limits of the range. It was then relatively easy to trade. We look at this period in detail.

Image 18: E-mini, hourly heikin ashi chart, June 12 to June 23, 2017

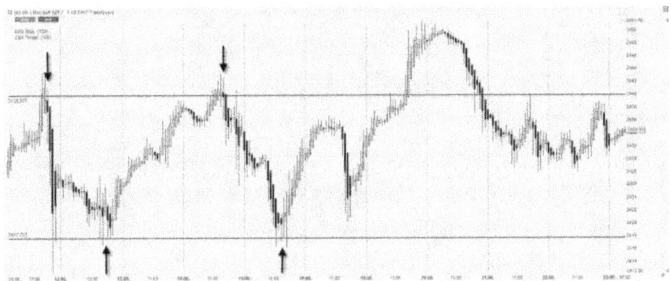

The arrows on the hour chart show again the tradable signals. There were two clear short signals (the arrows on the top), both of which hit their target (the lower range line). The two long signals were also profitable. The second signal (the arrow at the bottom right) did not hit the target price initially, but the trade was never really in danger.

One could say that I did not interpret the first touch with the support (far left in the chart) as a signal. It happened so fast that there was hardly the opportunity for a swing trader to trade this. You do not have to take any signal.

After the second long signal hit the price target, the market broke up the upper limit, so that the trader expected a successful breakout. Under these circumstances, the trader should not go short. It was not until the next day that the market turned back into range.

Image 19: E-mini, hourly chart heikin ashi, June 23 to July 7, 2017

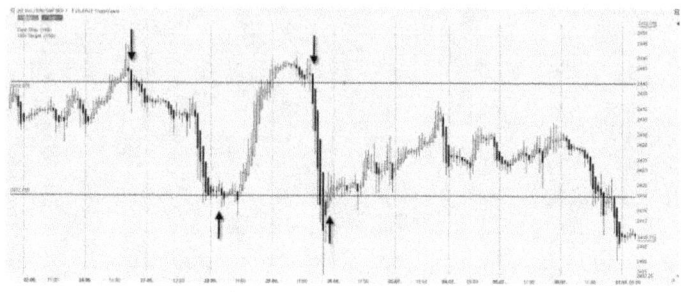

In the next section of the same period, there were four signals, two long and two short. The first three hit the target easily.

At the first short signal (the arrow in the upper left corner), the market broke the resistance line in the short term, but then formed a spinning top, whereupon it moved back into the range.

A similar scenario arose with the second short signal. Here the market demanded some patience from the trader, but finally, also a spinning top signaled that the buyers did not have the necessary strength to keep the market permanently above the resistance.

The first long signal (the arrow at the bottom left) came after the market had hit the bottom of the range. Here two dojis appeared, which caused the long signal. However, it still took several hours before the E-Mini moved up again. You can also see a small slider down. Anyone who had put the stop too tight here was probably out of the market. This is, of course, a classic case of a deception or fake, which I will discuss when it comes to the issue of stop setting and risk minimization.

At the second long signal, the market fell short of the support. A trader should observe this exaggeration and then buy in the subsequent hours at the support. Some dojis and spinning tops gave plenty of opportunities to do this. As long as the heikin ashi candles are in black (or red), there is no reason for me to buy. Only when the trader observes the downtrend weakening and the market returns to the range should he consider a long position.

I hope you can see that this method is not about a rush. If I miss a signal, I know that the next signal will always come. It is very important to carry out this type of trading with care. You should only act when there is a clear signal.

The second buy signal (the arrow at the bottom right) did not lead anywhere. There was no loss, but if a market like this daylong goes sideways without even reaching the other side of the range, it is better in my experience to close the position gradually or to outscale it completely.

The trader can out scale the position as follows. Let's say the trader had bought three E-mini contracts. After the market went up after two trading days but then fell back again, he could to sell the first contract (with a small profit). The next day, the market ran sideways again without hitting the upper limit (the target). Here, he could sell the second contract and set the stop loss to break even. If you have been in the market for three days without hitting the price target, the risk management should come in. With the last contract, the trader now has the choice to either wait until the market hits the breakeven-stop or set the stop even closer to the market.

I tend to the second variant. Not because I do not trust my method (after all, the target could be hit anyway), but from the experience that the longer a trade needs, the less likely that the price target is actually hit. Rather, the opposite happens, as this example demonstrates.

However, there is also a more important reason you should consider outscaling in such cases. Hardly anything stresses the nerves of a trader more than a market that leads nowhere. Of course, there is always the chance that the trade finally leads to success, but this will be smaller every day. That is why it is better to end the trade and try something new.

You will experience markets that give the trader a "small" profit without ever hitting the price target. As you can clearly see, closing the position was the better option, as a few days later the market fell below the support line.

C. Deeper Examination of a Sideways Period in the FDAX

20: FDAX, 4 hours bar chart, March 24 to August 2, 2017

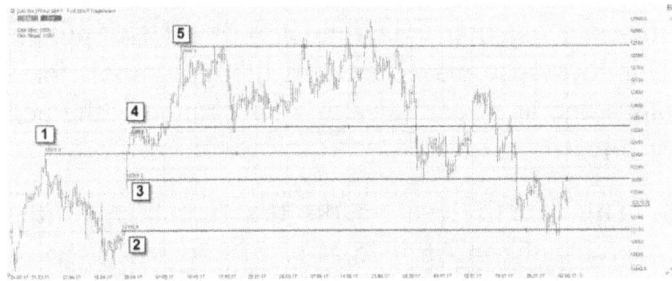

If we look at this 4-hour overview chart for the DAX futures, some striking levels are worth mentioning. On the left side of the chart, I have marked five points that represent five price levels that played an important role in the weeks and months that followed and were still playing at the time of the screenshot (August 2, 2017).

1. The first price level shows a significant high at 12,413 points on April 3, 2017, from which a downward wave started. Later in July, it played a role as support of a range.

2. The second price level shows the closing price of Friday, April 21, 2017 at 12.099 points. It was the Friday before the first round in the 2017 French elections. After the candidate Emmanuel Macron won on Sunday, April 23, the FDAX opened on Monday with an upward gap (Macron-Gap) of 185 points. In the course of the day, the FDAX rose continuously and the closing price was exactly the high at Level 1.

3. The third price level shows the opening price after the election (Macron-Gap) at 12.305 points. This level also played later in July as support for a range and as a resistance to a later range at the end of July.

4. The fourth level marks the first high of the Macron rally on April 25 at 12,518 points. It served as a resistance of the July 1 range.

5. The fifth level marks the preliminary high of the "Macron-Rally," which started on April 24. This high was on May 5 at 12,841 points, and the market still did not take out this level at the time of the screenshot (August 2, 2017).

These four "events" will determine the playing field for the FDAX in the coming weeks. We recognized the gap of April 24 in technical analysis as a "Runaway Gap." This means that the buyers are so dominant that they surprise the sellers and rally the market without a look back.

Now the "Macron-Rally" was actually good for 700 points in the FDAX. However, it was still difficult to trade, because the trader would have had to open a long position on the Friday before the election. He should therefore have speculated that Macron would actually win the first round and that the market would respond positively. The forecast predicted this scenario before Election Day. However, what would have happened if the result for Mr. Macron had not been so favorable? If the opponent Le Pen had won a favorable result, which would have given her a realistic perspective to win the second round? Would the FDAX in this scenario have opened with a gap down of 185 points? A stop loss would not have helped. The trader would have had to pay a big loss in this case.

This is also one of my criticisms of trading trends. In this case, the trend trader must work with stops that he puts far from the current price. In other words, to trade the Macron rally of 700 points, the trader should have a minimum stop distance of 200 points; otherwise, he would risk the market pulling him out by a random countermove. Now, risk/reward ratios of 2:7 are still very good. However, very few traders would be able to trade this with a DAX future. Most traders would need financial instruments with a lower leverage, such as an ETF on the DAX.

In other words, trading this kind of trend is quite feasible, but the trader should then at least trade with the 4-hour chart or even better with a daily chart. I call such a method swing trading., I have described how to do this in my three-part series, "Swing trading with the 4-hour chart."

The traders, who had missed the Macron rally (most of them) now had the problem that they would get into a market environment that is engaged in "digesting" the Macron rally.

After the FDAX made the first swing high of 12,842 points on May 5, he went for weeks in a trading range with a fluctuation margin of just 200 to 250 points. The Macron rally was therefore again the exception, while the range, which followed, formed the rule.

The FDAX tried to conquer the high from May 5 a number of times, but this happened only in the short term as the false breakouts on the upper horizontal resistance line clearly show. Therefore, if the trend trader hoped that the market would continue the Macron rally by trading breakouts, he would have to close his positions after a few hours with a loss. We see that the FDAX came back 200 points after each breakout attempt and thus confirmed and strengthened the range.

Overall, there were more than 10 attempts to break the upper resistance of 12,842 points. At the time of the screenshot, the FDAX had still not managed to break this resistance. Since it requires at least two touches so that the trader can identify a trading range as such, the first two do not represent signals for the range trader. Only starting from the third touch, he could have opened a short position with price target support. There were eight of them, seven of which had made profits. The breakout of June 19, however, was successful, even if the market went back into the range the next day.

The range lasted for two months, while the "Macron-Rally" just took nine trading days. This illustrates the fact that trend movements usually take little time, whereas in most cases the markets are not in a trend movement. The question is, of course, can a trader profit on any of these important trend movements, and get on and off on time in the market?

If you can answer this question clearly with "yes," then congratulations: I recommend that you become a trend trader. If the answer is "no," then I urge you to question your intention to trade "trends" in the markets.

Image 21: FDAX, 4-hour chart, May 5 to May 25, 2017

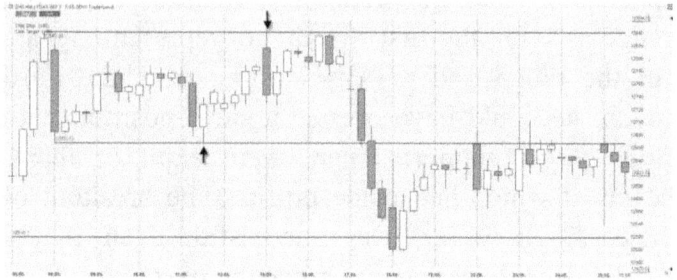

In the example shown above in Image 21, the two arrows show the moment when the market confirmed the range. From this moment, the trader had a clear "playing field." The upper limit was still the high of May 5, 2017 at 12,840. For the lower limit (the red horizontal line center), it took two lows on the 4-hour chart at a price of 12,667. In other words, the trading range of the FDAX was just 174 points wide. However, this is sufficient for a good range trader to get profitable signals.

The market confirmed the range with the next touch (the arrow on the top) a few hours later. Interestingly, the buyers did not really touch the resistance level at 12,840. Two points were missing. If you see something like this as a trader, you get interesting information from the market. Buyers seem not to have the power (and the money) to even hit the resistance line, which points to a momentary weakness of the buyers. Actually, a few hours later, the market went in the other direction. Is this information sufficient for a short trade?

For me, it is not. I would like to have a confirmation on the resistance line, which shows me the "exhaustion" of the bulls. Since this was missing, I did not take a short position.

The DAX then took a dive into the south and quickly hit the lower limit of the range at 12,666 (red line). Should I take a buy position here as a range trader? Again, the simple touch with the support line is not enough to trade. I would like to see a confirmation of the market that the train will soon take off again in the other direction.

As you can see clearly, this confirmation did not occur, but the DAX fell even below the lower limit of the range. So if you had gone blue-eyed long here, you would have been eaten alive by the bears. The FDAX did not go anywhere, however arbitrarily. He pretty much hit the first high of the Macron rally at 12,518 (the horizontal blue line below). Actually, he went a few points below the round number 12,500. However, we can see clearly that the market turned here.

Image 22: FDAX, hourly chart Heikin Ashi, May 17 to June 1, 2017

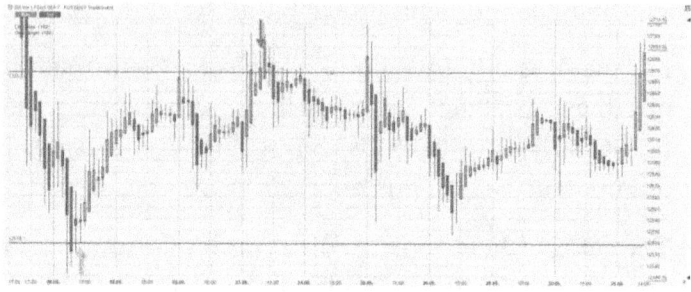

We zoom a little further into the chart and now look at the hourly chart for a period of about two weeks, in which the FDAX remained under the red centerline (above).

After slipping to the blue line below (the first high of the Macron rally) at 12,518, the market turned and formed in the hourly chart a spinning top that marks a balance between buyers and sellers. Here one could have taken a long position (the green arrow below) with a target price of 12,666, thus the red middle line. The DAX reached this goal.

There were three touches with the red resistance line, but of the three short signals, only one (the red arrow above) got an execution. Unfortunately, this trade did not hit the price target and the trader had to take out of the market with a small loss.

After that, the FDAX stayed within the trading range and made only a short signal, without execution.

Image 23, FDAX, hourly chart, June 1 to June 22, 2017

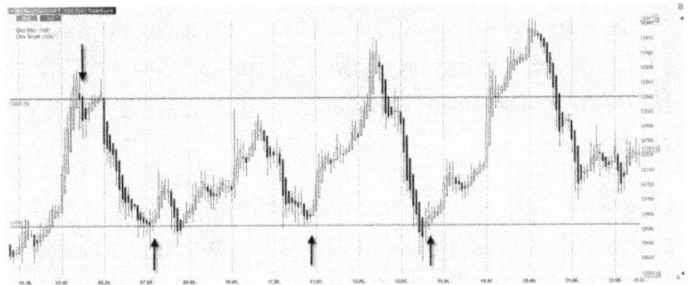

After the FDAX had recaptured the red central line on June 1, 2017, we got some tradable signals again. A short signal came on June 2 (the left arrow on the top) after the FDAX had reached the high of the Macron rally at 12,840. After the market had just shot over this high, it made a spinning top, which triggered the short signal at this point. The trader could go short at the upper limit of the range without forgetting that the market could resume the "Macron-Rally" at any time.

The better chances were clearly on the long side. We got three buy signals (the three arrows at the bottom), all three were profitable. Only the first signal (the arrow at the bottom left) did not hit the target (the upper horizontal line). The other two even exceeded it.

We must regard the two breakouts above the upper limit as successful, even if they turned out to be false outbreaks later. The trader could not know this at the moment of the breakout. Therefore, it is always better to wait for a clear signal of weakness at the upper boundary. This did not occur in the first hours after the breakout. That is why I would not go short here.

Overall, the deeper consideration of a longer sideward phase in the FDAX shows that this can result in several interesting trading signals, provided the trader has the patience to wait for them. What is decisive is, of course, the trader is able to "look to the left in the chart."

10. Advanced Strategies

A. Opportunistic Limits
If you master the basic strategy of range trading, perhaps one day the time will come to think about more advanced strategies. Although the basic strategy, properly applied, can be very profitable, it makes sense to deal with methods that you might not have tried at first.

One of these methods is the use of so-called "opportunistic limits." An opportunistic limit is a "bargain price," in which the execution price is clearly below the last traded price. In the case of a short position, the execution price is clearly above the last traded price.

Traders, who like to work with this kind of limit order, speculate on short-term price outliers down or up. Markets usually come back to the mean again within a short time. The classic case is the already mentioned flash crash, in which sellers suddenly sweep up the order book off the market and there are no buyers. The market then usually breaks down within minutes until it reaches a low level at which buyers catch it up again.

This was the case, for example, in the American Index SP500 on May 6, 2010. Within six minutes, the index fell by 6%. In the index, Dow Jones Industrials, the drop was even more than 9%, which led to a loss of almost 1000 points! A previously unseen event. Some shares lost over 99% of their value in the short term.

Equally spectacular was the flash crash of October 7, 2016 in the British pound. Here it was 10% against the US dollar. However, the pound was able to recover quickly and reduce the loss to 1.5%.

An extreme event occurred in the crypto currency Ethereum. The price of this financial instrument dropped on June 21, 2017 within a few minutes from US $296 to US $13 to recover completely.

The reasons for such extreme events may be different. The fact is that a financial market implodes because of an imminent shortage of buyers, or a surplus of sellers.

Such events, however, are difficult or impossible to predict. They also occur so rarely that it is almost impossible to profit from them.

Now the "drop" does not always have to be so extreme. Occasional slips down or up happen in every market, and there is, in my opinion, a method to benefit from it. Especially if a market is in a sideways tendency.

Instead of being the victim of such a drop (the exaggeration takes the stop-loss order of the range trader out of the market), the trader could turn the tables and speculate on these outliers. Instead of placing a limit buy on the support line (or limit sale on the resistance line), he would wait until a slip occurred and place a limit buy far under the support line in the hope that a short break would execute the order.

Therefore I call this type of order an "opportunistic limit," because the trader is not satisfied with the current price but wants to go into the market for a better price. The trader goes so to speak under the "bargain hunters."

Now it has never been wrong, as in other places in life, to try to get a cheaper price for something that is actually worth more. In many countries, merchants even consider haggling as an accepted practice.

I myself belong to this species as a trader. For example, since I travel a lot, I take special pleasure in never paying the holiday price proposed by the property owner (which is usually inflated), but vigorously bid under the "market price."

Once I managed to get a beautiful ocean view apartment in the center of Larnaca in Cyprus for 400 euros for four weeks. The pledge came after I had received only eight cancellations from other property owners (or no answer). Normally the apartment would cost about 1200 euros. They even offered me a gratis taxi from the airport into the center. When I checked in, the sympathetic manager of the apartment block looked at me with a how-did-you manage-to-get-this-price look. His daughter had accepted my bid online, and when he gave me the key, I could literally feel that he was gritting his teeth: "Once, but never again."

In reality, he hadn't rented even half of his apartments during my stay there. Therefore, he had a choice: stay stubborn and hold on to his prize or take my 400 euros. His daughter decided to take the 400 euros.

This simple business principle is valid in all areas of life. On the stock exchange, however, I often have the impression that traders like to pay 1200 euros and even a bit more. They might think: well, if this is the price that is in the catalog, it will probably be right.

Unfortunately, this naive mentality is an expensive pleasure. Often their stop-loss orders are executed at exactly the price at which they should have had to place their opportunistic limit. In short, the pros have pulled off their pants.

Now this kind of bargaining does not always work, and the price keeps well over the support line. Well, then you do not get a position. It is that simple.

Some traders seem to have a problem with this: no position. They want to always have a position, whatever it costs.

My suggestion, however, is to be a bit more stingy and prefer to pass on a position than to buy too expensive. I know it is not everyone's taste, but it is usually more profitable. As an example, I would like to show some opportunistic trades in the EUR/USD.

Image 24: EUR/USD, 4-hour chart, May 19 to June 13, 2017

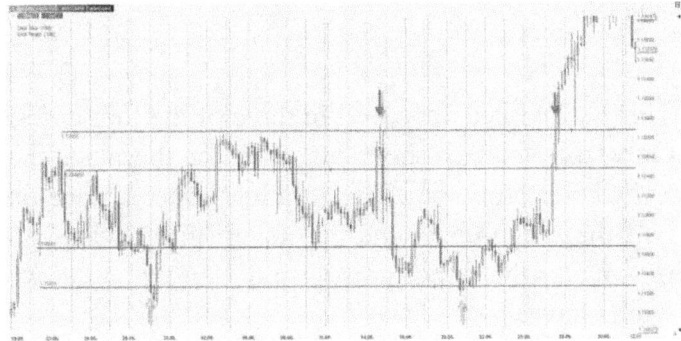

You may not recognize the trading range at first sight (the two inner blue lines). They were overall good for a range of 80 pips in EUR/USD. The red upper and the red bottom line are the levels where I had placed "opportunistic limits." I usually select half of the range (in this case, 40 pips) for the opportunistic limits. This is the level at which most "slip-ups" happen with trading ranges, in my experience.

If I had traded the basic method, the market would have stopped me out with a loss a few times. The market executed the opportunistic limit four times; two buy positions (green arrows at the bottom) and two short positions (red arrows at the top).

The price target is the opposite limit of the range, as we have pointed out in the basic method. In the case of a buy positions the upper limit or the resistance. For a short trade, we aim for the lower limit or support.

This has worked very well in three of the four cases. Only the second short hit the stop because the EUR/USD broke out. The stop loss order I place on half the range under the buy level (in this case, 40 pips under the opportunistic limit). In this case, we would have:

3 winning trades: 3 x 120 pips = 360 pips

<u>1 losing trade: 1 x 40 pips = 40 pips</u>

Net total   320 pips

Image 25: EUR/USD, 4-hour chart, May 19 to June 13, 2017 (Basis method)

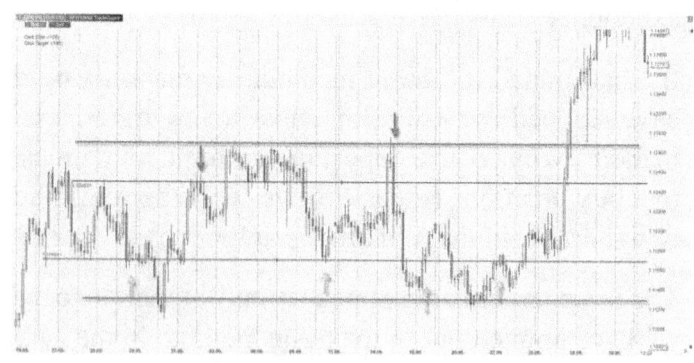

If the trader had acted with the basic method, he would have received six trading signals instead of four: four long signals and two short signals. Of the four long signals, two hit the target and two hit the stop (the bottom red line). The two short signals hit the price target. Here, too, we look at the results:

Four winning trades: 4 x 80 pips = 320 pips

Two losing trades: 2 x 40 pips = 80 pips

Net total: 240 pips

I would be quite satisfied with this result. However, if you compare it with the opportunistic limit method, you would have bet on this one because the results are even better. In addition, the opportunistic method needed only four trades to achieve a much better result, and the risk/reward ratio is better: 1:3.

The disadvantage of the opportunistic method is, of course, that the trader will not always get an execution. The question is whether this is really a disadvantage if it occasionally saves you from losing trades.

I know some readers will be confused by this "opportunistic alternative." The question might well emerge: what is better now? The basic method or the opportunistic-limit method?

I think the answer is almost a philosophical one. What kind of trading philosophy do you prefer? A philosophy that accepts the current price and insists that stop-loss, risk/reward ratio, and hit rate will do the hard work for you?

On the other hand, do you prefer the "scrooge philosophy," which means that the market occasionally gives you a discount? Scrooge traders must, of course, be patient traders, because it can take a long time before the discount happens or it may not even occur at all.

It would be possible to combine both methods. In this case, the trader would trade support and resistance without ifs and buts, but at the same time, he would place an additional opportunistic limit in case the market occasionally makes a slip.

The combination of both methods naturally leads to more trades. If you start with the basic method, you occasionally get a second chance thanks to the opportunistic limit.

B. Fakeouts

The fakeout (false breakout) I call a variant of the opportunistic limit, although it is here something else going on. A fakeout is nothing more than a deception maneuver, which some market participants stage in a market. They are quite frequent in range markets, because liquidity is lower than usual here. It is therefore relatively easy to make such a fakeout for a middle-sized market player. An example may illustrate the phenomenon.

Image 26: GBP/USD, hourly chart, April 20 to April 23, 2017

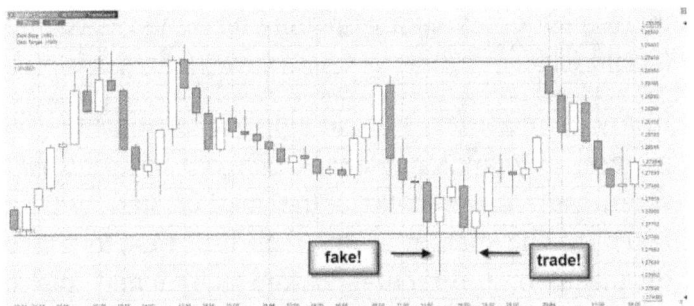

On April 21, 2017, the market fell short of the range (fakeout) in order to return to the range within the same hour. This is happening quite frequently and might be a chance for a smart range trader. However, it is not a matter of trying to trade the fake itself. When it occurs, the trader can place a limit buy on the support line. The probability that the market executes the order is usually high.

However, the trader could try to place a limit order slightly lower, for example, half the height of the fake candle. Frequently, fake candles just do not appear alone. Often you can observe more activity around the fake candle as in the example in the GBP/USD. In this case, two hours later, another smaller fake candle occurred that executed the waiting order slightly under the support line.

If the trader can achieve this successfully, he usually gets a very favorable price into the market. The market executed the take profit order only after the weekend, i.e., at the opening on Sunday evening (23.00 CET).

In my opinion, fakes are among the most profitable patterns in today's markets. Often you will find that significant movements in the market start with a fakeout. The market seems therefore first to move in the wrong direction before the actual move comes. It is as if some market players once again want to get into the market at really cheap prices before they drive it upward (or downward at downtrends).

If you are interested in fake trading, I recommend the second part of my book: "Swing trading with the 4-hour chart." In this volume "Trade the Fake," I will go into the topic in detail and show how to develop a very profitable strategy based entirely on fakes.

11. Trend Channels (Channel Trading)

The trader community understands range trading usually as a variant of the broader term "channel trading." What do I mean by that?

Channel trading is the name of any type of trading where two equidistant lines have a range of resistance and a range of support. The equidistant lines can run horizontally as we have seen in the range trading. They can also be ascending or descending. In this form, of course, they mark some kind of trend behavior and therefore we speak of a <u>trend channel</u>.

Many trading platforms already have tools for the automatic drawing of trend channels. If you can connect significant lows to each other in a trend, the resistance line is automatically equidistant. The trader usually needs to make some adjustment in order to identify the channel.

If you study trend channels, you might conclude that they are much more common than you would expect. Moreover, the market players seem to stick to the touch of the trend channel. That is why I believe that channel trading or trading with trend channels is definitely part of the repertoire of a range trader. While horizontal ranges are easier to recognize at first glance or perhaps easier to trade, they do not occur as often as trend channels.

Image 27: AUD/USD, hourly chart, February 7 to February 28, 2017

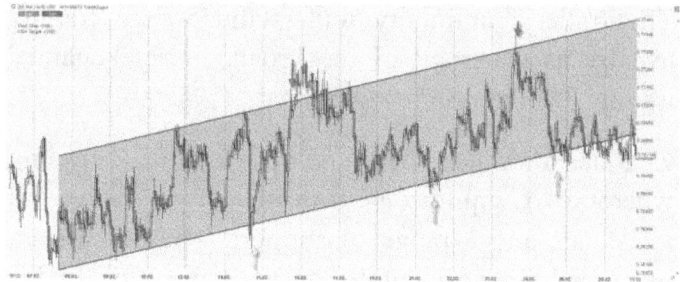

I discovered a trend channel in this hourly chart of the AUD/USD pair, which might not be apparent at first sight. Only the higher highs that formed the bottom of the canal marked a gently rising trend in this market.

Trading trend channels is somewhat more difficult compared to range trading because the price target cannot be determined exactly. The principle is similar to range trading: buy at the support line with a target resistance line and vice versa.

If you draw horizontal lines, finding the target is easy. If the lines are equidistant but ascending, the trader cannot know at which point the market will hit the upper limit of the trend channel. He can estimate it, but this estimate is by no means certain. The market may take longer to reach the price target. This means, of course, that he cannot work with bracket orders. He must exit (close) the trade manually.

In order to prevent this shortcoming, the trader could nevertheless work with a take-profit order and set it to "ambitious," which is somewhat higher than his estimate of the price at which the market will reach the upper limit of the channel. As soon as the trade begins to move in his favor, he can adjust the take-profit order manually.

In the example shown in Image 27, there were a total of five tradable signals, three long signals, and two short signals. The first two long trades hit the price target. The third trade the trader had to take out of the market because of lack of a trend, with either a small loss or break-even.

The first short trade ended in a loss, or hit the price target, depending on the stop. As far as the stop is concerned, I go the same way as with range trading. I set the stop at 50% of the range of the channel. In this case, the fluctuation width was 63 pips. I thus put the stop at 32 pips above the entry. The second short position hit the price target.

For the setup to be clear, I will present a trade in the USD/CAD currency pair:

Image 28: USD/CAD, daily chart, October 9 to December 21, 2016

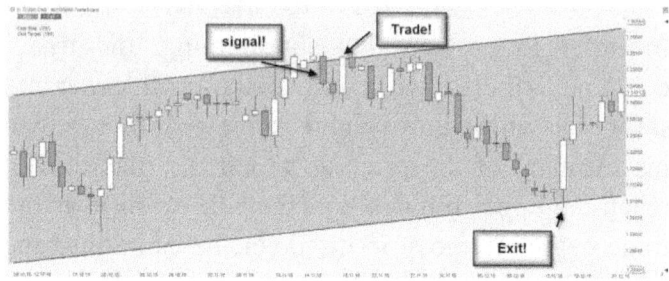

On the daily chart, the pair hit the upper limit of the trend channel on November 11, 2016 and closed above the channel. During the next two trading days, the pair stayed above the upper boundary of the canal. However, the candle of the second day formed a pin bar. This was a first indication that the "breakout" over the channel would probably fail, which then happened with the red candle the next day (signal, arrow left above). This candle formed the short signal. Only then, was the trader able to place a limit sell order with the support line of the channel as a target. The execution of this order did not occur on the same day, but the next day, when the pair again attacked the upper limit with a white candle (on Nov 17, 2016).

The market hit the take profit order on Dec 14, 2016 (the arrow at the bottom). The trade was good for 450 pips.

Should you not trade with the trend when you are dealing with trend channels? The answer seems obvious: yes. However, this is not my experience. As the above example shows, the USD/CAD trend was up. Nevertheless, you could make good money with a short position. We call trend channels trend channels because the price stays within a channel. This means nothing else but that the chances are on both sides.

This also applies to the breakout from the trend channel, which can occur at any time and ends the channel. This breakout can happen in the direction in which the trend channel points. However, very often the opposite happens. Therefore, one should not speculate on this or that output, but just trade the channel and nothing else.

From a psychological point of view, this is perhaps the greatest advantage of range trading and trend channel trading: entry, stop, and price target are clearly defined.

My experience is that many starting traders may spend months, in some cases even years, figuring out where to buy (or sell), where to put the stop, and where to close the trade (take profit). Again, I emphasize that such questions are what they are: beginner questions.

The advantage of range trading is quite clear: it answers all these questions from the very beginning. Because it is the range itself that answers them.

12. What Is Really Important

What questions should a trader deal with, if they are not the (seeming) important: entry, stop, and exit? My answer is this: every experienced trader deals with the really important questions, namely:

1. What is the average profit of my winning trades?

2. What is the average loss of my losing trades?

3. How high (or low) is the hit rate of my system?

4. What is the payoff ratio (the ratio between average profit and average loss?)

5. Finally, how much profit can I expect from each trade I enter? What is the expectancy of my trading system?

I have dealt extensively with these five parameters, which decide on the profitability of a trading strategy in the third part of my scalping series "Scalping is fun!" Here I introduce a trader named Jenny, who I have accompanied over 12 weeks. The book deals exclusively with the five questions mentioned above.

You can earn money as a trader if the answer to question five is positive: can the trader expect a statistically positive result for every trade he enters? Not for every trade, but on average? The other four questions then relate to the level of this expectation.

In addition, you can optimize a trading system to increase profitability. I have tried to demonstrate how you can do this using Jenny's scalping strategy.

With the range and channel strategy, traders have the great advantage of being able to deal with the five important questions of trading. In other words, the chance exists that the learning curve of such a trader can go faster than is usually the case.

Now some readers might ask whether range trading is compatible with my Heikin Ashi scalping system. The answer is, of course, it does!

Almost nowhere does the Heikin Ashi countertrend scalping work better to your advantage than using the principle of support and resistance in a range (or in a channel). Here again is the example from June 2017 in the FDAX (see also Image 23).

Image 28, FDAX, hourly chart, June 1 to June 22, 2017

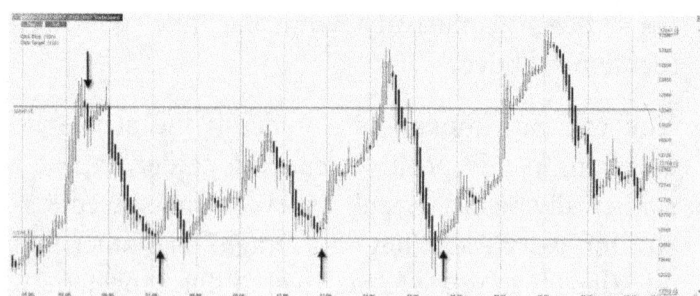

In this example, a trader using the heikin ashi candles, who specializes in trading ranges, got four well tradable signals (the arrows in the chart). Of course, the market sometimes goes further than the target, as the two false breakouts over the upper limit of the range (right in the chart) clearly show. However, here a smart trader, who works with opportunistic limits, could have a real advantage. Anyone who would have gone short twice, as soon as the color of the heikin ashi candles changed from green to red, would have earned an even greater profit than if he had merely traded the range itself.

The use of heikin ashi candles can give your range trading an extra boost. The trader has an additional confirmation at the moment the color changes on the support line or on the resistance line. This makes the trading signal stronger. If the color change occurs outside the range, the trader often gets even better signals.

13. Range Trading for Day Traders and Scalpers

After reading my views about range trading in the area of the hour and the four-hour chart, people often wonder whether the strategies mentioned could apply to shorter periods. In other words, can day traders and even scalpers benefit from this method?

The answer is a clear "yes." It is a peculiarity of the financial markets that the way they develop patterns is possible on each time level. It is also of great importance that traders who move on shorter time frames do not neglect the higher time frames. For it is the players on the higher time levels that ultimately move the market. To illustrate this, let's look at the hourly chart of the FDAX from July 3 to July 21, 2017.

Image 30: FDAX, hourly chart, July 3 to July 21, 2017

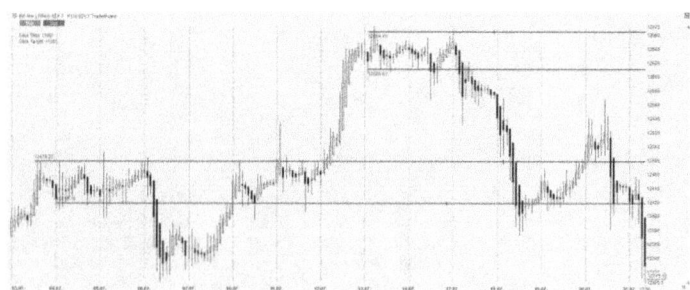

This chart illustrates once again the fact that the market is predominantly in a "sideways" mode, while the trend periods are rather short. Of course, there are exceptions where markets can move (or fall) a few weeks or even one to two months. Often one will then experience that after such a movement, they are consolidating trendless for months. That is why we should deal with these "trendless periods."

Another interesting phenomenon that shows the above chart is the fact that markets like to go back to established ranks, even after they had left them for a few days (or weeks). You can see it on the left side of the chart where the FDAX leaves the range on the 6th and 7th July to reach it again after the weekend on July 10 (and to respect!).

Then followed an upward move (on July 12), after which the DAX went sideways two days later (July 13–14). Thereupon, on July 17 and 18, a downward movement brought the DAX back into the range from July 4 to July 6, as if nothing had happened.

A day trader, who occasionally looks at the hourly chart, would have observed this behavior. He would at least have some indications for the highs and lows of his trading day.

Such a recapture of an old range happens more frequent than you might expect. Markets may be able to "recall" an old sideways range weeks later, in extreme cases up to one or two months.

Therefore, if you want to get to know your "day trading market" a little bit more, I really recommend you watch the action on the hourly chart and on the 4-hour chart. You will find astonishing coincidences that could help you determine possible pivot points when day trading. If you use such instruments as heikin ashi charts, you have good chances to identify precise entries (and exits) on a 5-minute chart. This is one of the most popular charts for day traders. We therefore look at an intraday chart for July 5, 2017.

Image 31: FDAX, 5-minute chart, July 5, 2017

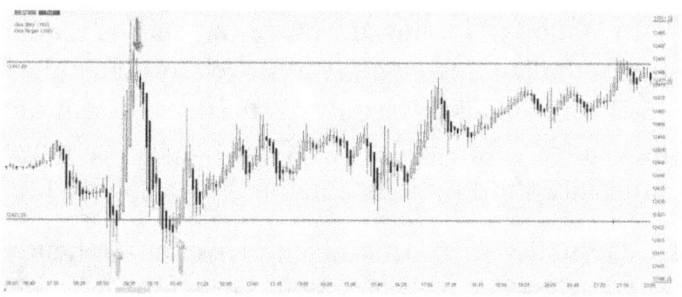

After a range was established on July 3 and July 4, which was good for about 60 FDAX points, a day trader could now also benefit from this knowledge and observe the events at the two limits of the range (horizontal lines).

We see on the 5-minute chart that the FDAX was at the lower limit of the range just before the opening of the stock exchange in Frankfurt (9.00 CET). Initially, he undercut the support in the short term, but none of the sellers' attempts proved to be sustainable. The closing price of the candles remained above the lower limit. This is, of course, an initial indication for the day trader that it might possibly go in the other direction. The upper limit of the range, 60 DAX points higher, would be the target for a possible upward movement. A few minutes later (shortly after the opening in Frankfurt) this move occurred and hit the target goal after 20 minutes.

The market shot over the target and tried "a breakout," which also turned out to be a "false breakout" half an hour earlier. The day trader again gets an important piece of information that the range could possibly continue to hold. Of course, you can never be sure about this. However, the heikin ashi candles showed two futile attempts to overcome the resistance; therefore the trader could open a short position at the resistance line with the target lower limit (the red arrow above). This idea also proved to be profitable, as half an hour later, the DAX was again exactly where it had started at the market opening (on the support line).

In addition, the market remained exciting. For the second time, the sellers tried to push the FDAX under the range, which failed again. This was another indication that a day trader could use to take another long attempt at the support line. Although this assessment proved to be correct, the FDAX did not hit the price target as fast as the first two times. It took until the close of trading (22.00 clock CET) until the FDAX finally hit the upper limit. Thus, a trader could realize three times 60 points in the FDAX, which corresponds to 4500 euros per traded contract.

In practice, I know that such (very late) targets in day trading are difficult to achieve. After all, the trader wants to take a break. You can still trade this by using more than one contract. If the FDAX is too expensive, you can always switch to the newly introduced mini-DAX future. As you can see, the market moved for the rest of the day within the range. For such cases, I recommend the scaling-out technique. If the trader is long with three contracts, he can sell the first contract at noon, a second after the opening of the American markets, and the third run with a stop at the entry.

Image 32: EUR/USD, 1-minute chart, July 21, 2017

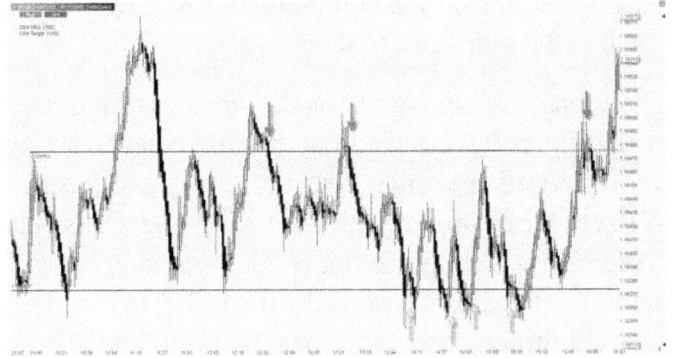

Scalping also has a lot to do with range trading. I would even say that scalping works very well here because the range clearly marks "the trading field" as you can see in the EUR/USD chart above. The range in this case was only 10 pips wide. I recommend trading such narrow ranges only if you have excellent conditions in Forex. Whoever pays a spread of one pip pays 10% of the range and should have a hard time trading it profitable.

However, if you only pay 0.2 or 0.3 pips, such a range scalping can be worthwhile, as the signals in the chart clearly show. Of the seven signals, only the third short signal (the red arrow in the upper right) resulted in a loss. Here the EUR/USD managed to break out of the range.

For the other signals, a scalper could make good money. However, in this example, several trades clearly did not hit the price target. Only two trades reached the other end of the range.

Therefore, we should consider that scalping is a very different game than day trading or even swing trading. A scalper must learn to take quick profits. We see, for example, with the four long signals (the green arrows, bottom right) that the market just made it to half the range. Either the heikin ashi candles turned into the black and soon fell back again or they consolidated a little, as was the case with the first buy signal (arrow left).

Even if the price target was the upper limit of the range, the scalper at this point should try to realize the gains. If the market gives him five pips, he should take five. If the market gives him three, then he should take three. Optimistically speaking, a good scalper can make 15 to 20 pips in such a market. Needless to say, if you do that with one or two mini lots ($10,000), you cannot earn your livelihood.

However, the risks at each position are very manageable. If the scalper risks only half of the range (5 pips), he risks only $50 for each traded standard contract ($100,000). Professional scalpers like to trade with a few million at such minimal moves. If such a scalper realizes 10 pips with 10 standard contracts, then he makes $1,000 profit that day. That looks more like a reasonable income.

Also, consider that the scaling-out techniques mentioned above are usually not working for scalpers. Scalping just means cutting a little bit from a market movement. Take what the market gives you and run away with the money. Even if the market moves another 10 points after your exited the trade. You will rarely be able to trade the whole move.

Image 33: EUR/CHF, 3-minute chart, July 21, 2017

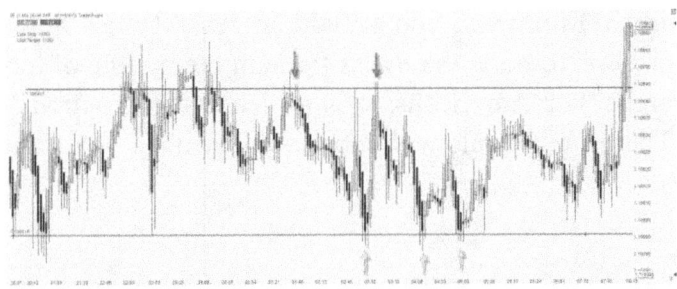

Very special scalping markets are the so-called "night markets in Forex." With "night," I mean here, of course, European night and US-American evening. Volatility in the forex is low at this time, and sometimes it is worth looking at the currency pairs, which mostly have a low volatility like the EUR/CHF or EUR/GBP.

Often these markets move in such narrow ranges that they hardly, or do not, leave them, as the above example shows in the EUR/CHF. This range was just 4.5 pips wide. This is, of course, out of the question for most traders, but smart scalpers with very good market conditions could take a serious look at such a market. After all, there were five signals in this example over a period of four hours, three of which hit the price target.

Certainly, such a thing is for very specialized people who operate in the market with large positions (starting at $1,000,000). In addition, if you are a European, you should at least be a "night person" to trade the Swiss franc in the middle of the night. For Americans, it is a nice evening activity. Therefore, people with jobs could try it.

Glossary

Equity index: Indicator for the performance of the stock market as a whole or individual equity groups (e.g. Dow Jones Industrials).

AUD/USD: Currency pair between the Australian Dollar and the US Dollar

Bond: Interest-bearing securities.

Bracket-Order: With a bracket-order, the trader can reduce the loss in advance and determine the amount of the potential gain

Breakeven: Profit threshold

Broker: Financial service provider who is responsible for the execution of the orders of investors

Candlestick: Representation of price changes based on a Japanese analysis technique

Commissions: Costs incurred in the purchase and sale of securities or futures contracts

DAX: German stock index

Day trading: Describes the short-term speculative trading of securities. Positions are opened and closed again within the same trading day, with the aim of benefiting from low price fluctuations.

Doji: Candlestick formation at which the opening and closing price are the same

Drawdown: Losses that can arise out of the peak within a certain time

E-Mini Future: Futures contract on the American Index SP500

Entry strategy: A strategy that determines the entry into a market

Expectancy: Indicator which shows the average of the results when the experiment is repeated indefinitely

EUR/CHF: Currency pair between the euro and the Swiss franc

EUR/GBP: Currency pair between the euro and the pound sterling

EUR/JPY: Currency pair between the euro and the Japanese yen

EUR/USD: Currency pair between the euro and the US dollar

Eurostoxx50 Future: Future on the stock index, which contains the 50 large listed companies of the Eurozone

Exit strategy: A strategy that determines the exit from a market

FDAX: Future contract on the German Stock Index (DAX)

Forex: Forex Exchange Market, international foreign exchange market

Futures: Futures contract – Standardized contract for the purchase or sale of a certain quantity of goods, at a fixed price, on a certain date

Gap: Price gap between two trading days

GBP/JPY: Currency pair between the British pound and the Japanese yen

GBP/USD: Currency pair between the British pound and the US Dollar

Heikin Ashi Chart: Japanese: "Balancing on a Foot." Japanese representation of price changes

Hit rate: The hit rate describes the ratio of profit trades to loss trades

Interest rate decision: Describes an event at which central banks announce the decision on the further course of interest rates

Learning curve: Describes the success rate of learning over the course of time in trading

Limit Order: Order with a fixed price and/or fixed time for execution

Liquidity: Describes the extent to which securities can be bought and sold at any time

Long: To be long is to buy and hold securities.

Lot: A lot is the trading unit for foreign exchange trading (Forex) and in futures markets. For Forex, a lot means a normal contract for 100,000 units of the front currency (basis), i.e., for the currency pair EUR/USD is one lot for US $100,000.

Money management: Money management is a value-added strategy that aims at controlling the risk of a securities portfolio by setting the size of the individual trading positions.

Pin bar: In the case of a pin bar, a preceding course movement in one direction is terminated and a new course movement is initiated in the opposite direction.

Pip: Percentage in point, smallest change in price in foreign exchange trading

Price target: A stock exchange price, which securities should reach because of an analysis

Range: Price area where a market goes sideways

Resistance: price level at which more sellers than buyers appear

Risk management: Includes all measures for the systematic identification, analysis, assessment, monitoring, and control of risks

Risk/reward ratio (RRR): The RRR serves as an indicator of the meaningfulness of an investment. It is calculated by dividing the expected profitability by the greatest possible loss (stop loss).

Round turn: Completed transaction where a security has been bought and resold

Scalping: Trading technique, in which the trader tries to trade minimal movements in the market

Short position: A trader is short when he sells a position without owning it (short selling)

Short signal: Trading signal that suggests a short sale

Slippage: The difference between the price charged and the actual price for the purchase of securities

Spinning Top: Chart pattern with a small body and long shadows

Spread: difference between buying and selling prices

S&P500 (Standard & Poor's 500): A stock index comprising 500 of the world's largest listed American companies

Stop Loss Order: Sales order, which is executed as soon as a certain price is reached

Support: The price level at which more buyers the sellers appear

Take Profit Order: Automated profit taking order, which is triggered as soon as a predefined price target has been reached

Tic: Smallest price change on a futures market

Time Stop: This order automatically closes a position after a predefined number of periods.

T-Note Future: Future on American government bonds with a maturity of 2, 3, 5, 7, and 10 years

Trailing Stop: Automatically traced stop-loss order

Trend following: Trading strategy, which is based on following a once-identified trend

USD/CAD: Currency pair between the US dollar and the Canadian dollar

USD/CHF: Currency pair between the US dollar and the Swiss franc

USD/JPY: Currency pair between the US dollar and the Japanese yen

Volatility: Standard deviation – indicates how much a price fluctuates

Other Books by Heikin Ashi Trader

How to start a Trading Business with $500

Many new traders have little capital available in the beginning, but this is not an obstacle to starting a trading career anyway.

However, this book is not about how to grow a $500 account into a $500,000 account. It is precisely these exaggerated return expectations that bring most beginners to failure.

Instead, the author shows, in a realistic way, how you can become a full-time trader in spite of limited start-up capital. This applies both for traders who want to remain private, as well as for those who want to eventually trade customer funds.

This book shows step by step how to do it. In addition, there is a concrete action plan for each step. Anyone can be a trader in principle, if he or she is willing to learn how this business works.

How to Scalp the Mini DAX Futures

Thanks to the introduction of the Mini-DAX futures (FDXM) private traders with smaller accounts are afforded the opportunity to scalp the German DAX Index to professional terms. Unlike most other trading instruments, Futures are the most transparent and effective way to make money in the financial markets.

Scalpers have infinitely more trading opportunities than position traders or day traders, which constitutes the real strength of this trading style. A scalper may therefore manage his capital much more effectively than all other market participants and thus achieve much greater returns than would otherwise be the case.

The Heikin Ashi Trader shows in this book how to successfully scalp this new future on the DAX. You will learn how to enter the market, how to manage your position and at which point you should back out. In addition, the book contains a wealth of tips and tools to make your trading even more effective and precise.

About the Author

Heikin Ashi Trader is recognized worldwide as the specialist in scalping with the Heikin Ashi chart. He has been trading this way for 19 years. He traded for a hedge fund and then went into business for himself as a trader. His scalping book "Scalping is Fun!" is an international bestseller and has been sold more than 30,000 times. You can find more information about his scalping method on his website www.heikinashitrader.net

With over 30,000 copies sold worldwide, the bestselling Heikin Ashi Trader book **"Scalping is Fun!"** is now an online course!

Discover how easy and fun scalping can be with the Heikin Ashi Trader method.

Skip the hassle of figuring out for yourself the fun way to trade. The "Scalping is Fun!" online course will help you enjoy scalping and be one step closer to financial freedom.

Join us in this course and avail yourself of the free workshop!

For more information, please visit:

www.scalpthemarkets.com

www.ingramcontent.com/pod-product-compliance
Lightning Source LLC
Chambersburg PA
CBHW070300230526
45470CB00002B/661